Panic AND Deaf

 General Editor, Howard Goldblatt

Fiction from Modern China

This series is intended to showcase new and exciting

works by China's finest contemporary novelists in fresh,

authoritative translations. It represents innovative recent

fiction by some of the boldest new voices in China today

as well as classic works of the twentieth century by

internationally acclaimed novelists. Bringing together

writers from several geographical areas and from a range

of cultural and political milieus, the series opens new

doors to contemporary China.

HOWARD GOLDBLATT
General Editor

Panic AND

TWO MODERN SATIRES

Deaf

Liang Xiaosheng

Translated by Hanming Chen

Edited by James O. Belcher

University of Hawai'i Press

Honolulu

Printed in the United States of America

06 05 04 03 02 01   5 4 3 2 1

Library of Congress Cataloging-in-Publication Data
Liang, Hsiao-sheng.
   [Novels. English. Selections]
   Panic and deaf : two modern satires / Liang Xiaosheng ; translated
by Hanming Chen ; edited by James O. Belcher.
      p.   cm. — (Fiction from modern China)
   ISBN 0–8248–2250–1 (alk. paper) — ISBN 0–8248–2373–7
      (pbk. : alk. paper)
   1. Liang, Hsiao-sheng, 1949—Translations into English.   I. Chen,
Hanming.   II. Belcher, James O.   III. Title.   IV. Series.
PL2878.A5974 A23 2001
895.1'352—dc21

00–057693

University of Hawai'i Press books are printed on acid-free
paper and meet the guidelines for permanence and
durability of the Council on Library Resources.

Designed by Trina Stahl

Printed by The Maple-Vail Book Manufacturing Group

Contents

Panic

Part One

MONDAYS — SO DIFFICULT to categorize. For people of wealth and leisure, Monday is Sunday's bonus. For others, who may be biding their time, Monday is the periscope of the armed submarine probing the calm ocean's surface. Some people start their week like a ferocious watchdog stepping out of its kennel; they focus their very reason for being upon the tasks at hand and accomplish half the week's work on Monday alone. You could say that Monday is *their* best friend. However, for some — specifically, those tragic individuals who are not cut out for exacting work but find it thrust upon them anyway, and the ones who loathe their supervisor, and let's also include the ones who simply were born under an unlucky star — for them, Monday is interrogation day. For all practical purposes, they may as well be newly paroled convicts who have completed their "education through labor" but must still appear at the police station for interrogation *every Monday*.

Yao Chun-gang despised Mondays. Actually, it was worse than that: he positively hated the day.

"*Hey* . . . You still sleeping?" Yao's wife gave him a nudge.

He didn't move, didn't open his eyes. He wanted to sleep some more. Well, no; actually, he had slept well and long enough and had even been awake for some time. He hadn't made love last night, even though his wife had dropped an unmistakable hint about her interest and hoped to kindle the same in him by snuggling up. He kissed her, fondled her, and the moment passed. It wasn't that he didn't want to do it. At one time, if the truth be known, Yao Chun-gang had possessed a robust sexual prowess. He could have serviced three wives; well, everybody carries around a few cherished memories. Last night, though, Yao had satisfied neither his wife nor himself. At first things were starting to happen, but then he remembered that the next morning would be Monday. Just the thought of the small, gray, two-story building where he worked—the place always looked to him like a tired, prematurely withered widow—or the thought of Executive Director Zhao Jing-yu with his potbelly and self-satisfied air and, well, Yao's manly virtues shrank to a lifeless vestige. *Ai, Monday!* How he hated Mondays.

"*Hey* . . . It's already past seven." His wife pushed him again.

Discipline had recently tightened at Yao's institute. For example, a carpenter had put up a card rack, and everyone was given a card with his or her name printed on one side. From that day on, the first task every morning was to flip one's card over, leaving it name side out. The face-out position indicated that the worker was on the job. A timekeeper checked the rack at the stroke of the hour to determine whether all had completed this task on time. Late arrivals had to file a statement in the personnel office, indicating the number of seconds or minutes they were late.

The directors were no exception. Yao was the second of the two directors.

The new rules of discipline had been promulgated by the

management; or more specifically, they had been thought up in Fat Zhao's brain and then announced by Yao to one and all. Fat Zhao liked to decide things. A third of his decisions were right; a third, wrong. The other third of the time he was an idiot. Some of Zhao's decisions were so irrelevant to everything on earth that Yao Chun-gang could not classify them. Nevertheless, Fat Zhao thought highly of his decisions, including the ones that were still under development.

After Fat Zhao had made the initial declarations about tightening up discipline at the work unit, it fell to Yao Chun-gang to inform the workers of the details of the executive director's decisions. That seemed to be the extent of Yao's managerial responsibilities, although Fat Zhao had never said as much to him. Nevertheless, the very idea humiliated and depressed Yao. *This world is so unfair,* he observed; *it always bows before power.* Yao asked himself why couldn't *he* do some of the deciding—and let Fat Zhao announce the details to the workers. Yao considered his mind to be much better than Fat Zhao's anyway, a full order of magnitude brighter. There had been lots of times when Yao came up with good ideas, but Fat Zhao either turned them down outright or smiled indifferently and said they'd talk about it later. Of course, he meant that Yao's ideas just weren't good enough to talk about *ever.* Yao Chun-gang had to face the facts: Fat Zhao had promoted him to assistant director to be a mouthpiece, a professional mouth to announce decisions as they bubbled up to the top of the director's head.

"A *director* must have an extraordinary brain! Why? So he can make decisions! A director whose brain can't make decisions is useless to the people." Zhao Jing-yu said these words, or something like them, every day. Sometimes he expressed the sentiment in large meetings, sometimes in small meetings;

sometimes he reiterated it privately to Yao. He was even known to mutter it aloud when he thought he was alone, as Zhao Jing-yu's kind is prone to do.

That said, whenever Zhao Jing-yu brought up the point about directors and their brains, Yao would listen with captive attention. He would gaze intently at Zhao as if committing a master's teachings to memory. Inside he was boiling with rage. How he wanted to give Fat Zhao a few choice slaps across the face! No matter how ordinary Zhao's comments might have been, it was obvious that he did not consider Yao's brain to be qualified for decision making at the executive-director level. Occasionally, in a fleeting moment of introspection, Yao might have been aware that Zhao never had *actually said* or *exactly implied* the slights that upset him so.

The previous Monday, just as Yao Chun-gang was announcing to the workers, ". . . and the directors are no exception!" Zhao Jing-yu interrupted him by rapping loudly on the tabletop several times. The executive director always interrupted his assistant that way, whether at public gatherings or in private discussion. Yao thought such behavior was unforgivably arrogant and rude. In all fairness, Yao did not consider Zhao to be an arrogant person; perhaps the director had never learned that interrupting people by pounding on the table was impolite. Either way, table pounding was totally inexcusable to Yao Chun-gang. Why couldn't the director simply say something like, "Excuse me, Chun-gang, may I interject something here?" And what would be so wrong if Zhao refilled Yao's water glass and handed him a cigarette before taking the floor? Yao always did that for him. At least the workers would think that the two administrators worked effectively together. The very thought of pouring water into Yao's glass had never occurred to Zhao, ever. Nor had he ever handed his assistant a cigarette. In fact, Zhao didn't ever leave his pack lying out on the table; the only time it came out of his pocket was when he lit up. In fairness to Zhao, the director was not a stingy person. Squirreling away his cigarettes was an unconscious habit. Yet all these things weighed heavily upon the assistant director. It was plain to see that he was all assistant and no director. His self-esteem languished. When an executive director interrupts his assistant by banging his fist on the table in front of so many people, it can only mean one thing: the executive director is flaunting his power over a subordinate. But then, how could anyone seriously blame Zhao Jingyu? The first time he interrupted that way, Yao accommodated him like a trained gorilla obeying its master's commands. Yao betrayed not a hint of the mortification he felt. You could only expect Yao's behavior to encourage Zhao's table-pounding habit.

It was last Monday that Zhao had interrupted his assistant to emphasize the point: "Yes—directors are no exception! And who is the director in this institute? Me!" He pointed to himself. Then he glanced at Yao. "Oh, and him, too. The same goes for both of us. I'm no exception; neither is he." Yao Chun gang smoldered in anger.

Zhao had begun his career in the military. After he retired, he transferred through a succession of work units. The directors at each unit hoped to take advantage of Zhao's experience as a military man and naturally always put him in charge of worker discipline. There is a common perception that military men are highly disciplined and therefore must be good at disciplining others. Zhao himself believed this. Moreover, his fellow managers were only too ready to hand over responsibilities that tended to make people unhappy. Zhao took such assignments to heart. He was strict—so strict that he didn't stay in any work unit for long. He saw nothing unusual about that. As far as he knew, it was standard operating procedure. His job was to serve the work unit and serve the Party.

At each of his jobs, Zhao was first to arrive in the morning and last to leave in the evening. Having a chauffeur drive him back and forth helped, but having a disciplined mind did, too. And even if you do have the means to get around quickly, you can still get bogged down by rush-hour traffic or an unlucky sequence of red lights because Beijing is a very crowded city. Zhao took such factors into account each day in deciding when he would leave for work. Allowing no exceptions for the directors posed no difficulty for him. To Zhao, it was exactly what Chairman Mao had taught: "Discipline is an arrow aimed at the heart of liberalism."

Compared to Zhao, Yao Chun-gang was a liberal, a slacker. Getting promoted to assistant director had forced Yao to modify some aspects of his behavior. Even so, he still missed the mark as a model for punctuality. He often arrived late and, once in a while, slipped out early. So it was plain to see that Zhao's "no-exception" pronouncement had been aimed directly at Yao. The shot across his bow, so to speak, came when Zhao penned the statement into Yao's draft of the announcement. Yao was mortified.

This Monday, Yao couldn't say why exactly, he suspected that Executive Director Zhao had worked up another decision somewhere in his brain. As soon as Yao got to his desk, there would lie the decision waiting to be announced to all the workers. His response to this suspicion was to stay in bed.

"Are you going to work today or not?" His wife was getting insistent. Instead of nudging him again, she pinched his arm.

Finally Yao opened his eyes. He retrieved his watch from under the pillow and peered at it: five to eight.

"I'm not going in." He jammed the watch back under his pillow and closed his eyes.

"Don't try to act like you don't know it's Monday!"

"Of course I know." He sensed that depression was going to overwhelm him.

"Well—did you ask for the day off?"

"No. Could you call Old Zhao for me?"

"What would I say to him?"

"Tell him I'm . . . sick."

"All right. What's wrong with you?"

"Anything that's going to keep me out of work today!" His eyelids were clenched shut.

"A cold? No, a cold and a fever."

"Nobody would have a cold in hot weather like this."

"Heatstroke."

"It's only eight in the morning. Who could have heatstroke?"

"Then . . . you have a stiff neck."

"I can't go to work because of a stiff neck?"

"Hmmm." His wife thought for a moment. "How about dysentery?"

Yao prodded her on with an inconclusive grunt.

"*Acute dysentery!*"

He kept his eyes closed, waiting for her to build a case. With the right twist, he might go with dysentery, even though there was something about the idea he didn't like.

"You were eating watermelon last night. It was rotten. You really ate a lot of it. So that's why . . ."

"Am I supposed to be that cheap? I was eating watermelon that I knew was rotten? And lots of it? A watermelon costs a couple of yuan. Come on!"

His wife was losing patience. "Then you tell me—why

aren't you going to work today? Want me to tell them you're too lazy to go in?"

While his wife pondered over selecting the most appropriate illness, Yao was racking his brains, too. He had always been healthy. If he weren't careful now, he would give himself away. Obviously he would have to steer clear of those chronic diseases that progress toward partial or total disability. They have a special name for those people: "old patients." Yao was only forty-five, still young enough to hope, or dream, that he could get promoted to executive director. They really look closely at a person's health when they're considering someone for promotion. Claiming the wrong disease today could be taking two steps backward to take one step forward. Yao could never let the report of an unacceptable disease get in the way of a promotion. He should not even think of going with some disgusting disease like hepatitis, psoriasis, or dysentery. People would be sure to keep their distance from him. Insomnia was more fashionable, but only intellectuals ever got that. Yao considered his thinking to be on a par with intellectuals, but the executive director of an institute must be careful not to put too much reliance on his brain. Besides, having a sleepless night now and then wasn't a good enough reason to miss work; and couldn't that make him look fragile? If he told them he had a history of insomnia, wouldn't people even get suspicious? *Why can't Yao sleep at night?* they would say. Their suspicions would surely ruin his credibility among the employees and his relationship with the director. Anemia would avoid those problems, but it was too feminine. The more Yao tried to think his way through all this, the more indecisive he became.

Now, there was a difference between the two men: Fat Zhao made decisions on impulse; Yao agonized.

The telephone rang. Yao's wife answered it: "Hello?" She instantly blanched and covered the receiver. "It's Old Zhao! He wants to know if you've left yet."

Yao froze. The instant surge of anxiety sparked an idea.

"Tell him . . . I've been fighting athlete's foot, but this morning it's really infected. It's so swollen, I can't walk. So I can't go to work."

"Old Zhao, Chun-gang's athlete's foot has gotten infected somehow. It's swollen so bad he can't walk." She paused a moment. "Um, before? . . ." His wife covered the mouthpiece again. "Old Zhao wants to know if it's ever been infected before!"

"*You* need to ask *me* about that?" He could hardly believe his wife's foolishness sometimes. What wife would have to ask her husband such a thing?

"*Don't look at me like that!*" she hissed. "Who's the one who ought to be rolling her eyes? It's none of my business. Here! Lie to him yourself!" She glared at him, lifted her fingers from the mouthpiece, and pushed the receiver into his hands.

The moment the receiver touched Yao's ear and he heard the voice at the other end, he became a different person. His manner was pleasant and sunny, utterly unlike that of the previous moment, much more like the watchdog that has just recognized its master's footsteps at the front door. Indeed, at precisely the same moment, Yao's wife envisioned him wagging his tail like a lapdog.

"Hello, this is Chun-gang," he said. "Thank you so much for your concern about me. I am touched, so touched. . . . Yes, yes, I can still walk, only . . . No, no, not a big deal, really . . . Well, I . . . They all say 'A foot is far away from the heart!' . . . Not at all; that's what an assistant is for . . ."

Yao hung up the receiver. "Damn! Old Zhao is sending his

personal car to pick me up. At least, I guess it means sometimes Zhao really does need me." He took a bit of comfort in musing on his usefulness to Zhao.

"Disgusting!" His wife gave a snort of contempt and rolled out of bed to get ready for work.

Yao rushed ahead of her to get to the bathroom first. The most important thing for him now would be to bandage a foot. He chose the left one and wrapped an entire roll of gauze around it.

His wife peered into the bathroom to watch him at work. After a while she said, "You brought it all on yourself."

He looked at the bandaged foot and began to pity it for the suffering it must endure in such hot weather. "What am I doing? Punishing myself!"

With his left foot in a slipper, he left home at 8:40 in the car Zhao Jing-yu had sent to pick him up.

THE CHINA PSYCHOLOGICAL History Research Institute had never found a definitive position within its administrative hierarchy. Sometimes the parent institutions paid it special attention by assigning to it various "talented persons" — individuals who had warranted a nice promotion but proved difficult to place. At other times no bureau wanted oversight responsibilities, leaving the institute forlorn as a motherless child. The China Psychological History Research Institute had been funded through an endowment that an overseas Chinese had set up a decade earlier. The principal was neither large nor small: five hundred thousand — U.S. dollars, of course; certainly not Chinese yuan. If it had been made in Chinese yuan, the fund would have dried up years ago. Ten years ago funds invested in hard currencies were earning very high returns. But not now; nowadays the yield from foreign funds had shrunk to a fraction of what it used to be. During the same decade, the staff at the institute had expanded from about ten to more than forty. The inevitable result was that the financial officer had been obliged to invade the principal repeatedly to balance the books.

To complicate matters, a robbery attempt some years before had left the director's office and the official records in such a shambles that the institute could no longer verify the conditions under which it had been established, or even which administrative body had approved the charter. Apparently, finding no cash on hand had exasperated the would-be thief. Anyone could understand that. He had spent a considerable amount of time casing the place, working out an elaborate plan, taking a huge, personal risk—and after all that, he was faced with no return on his investment of cunning and patience. Fortunately for the employees of the institute, the thief did not decide to burn the place down. Instead, he only trashed it. He broke all the telephones, took all the personnel files off to nobody knows where—presumably out of pure spite—and finished by leaving a pile of poop. None of the workers got too upset about the robbery, except the executive director, of course, who was observed gritting his teeth fiercely over the foul mess in his office.

Individually some of the workers were suddenly elated as unexpected opportunities presented themselves. Now, with no documentation to the contrary, anyone could shamelessly claim to have been a somebody all along—somebody recognized in the past with prestigious honors—and they had a perfect cover: the official records had, sadly, been destroyed by a madman. Unfortunately, genuine credentials awarded by supportive senior officials and endorsements made by public celebrities had disappeared along with the personnel files. To make matters even worse, the overseas Chinese patron died soon after the break-in, effectively ending any hope of replenishing the endowment principal. Of those who had originally commended the institute for its good work, only two were still alive. Two clerks of the institute were immediately sent to call on them and reestablish ties. The elderly comrades couldn't remember writing endorsements for anything called the China Psychological History Research Institute. Both suspected that someone had forged their names, and demanded repeatedly to see the documents for themselves. Being unable to produce the original documents, and not daring to admit they had in fact been stolen, the clerks were too abashed to solicit any kind of support, even psychological comfort.

These events sealed the institute's status as an orphan. All of the nurturing arms into which it so dearly wanted to throw itself were now folded tightly shut, for such an institute could only be an expensive burden. The few organizations that expressed any willingness to take over the institute had transparent designs on the principal that remained in the endowment. In view of such disasters, the executive director concluded that the institute had no future and deftly arranged his transfer to another work unit. Soon after that, a few of the staff left to start their own businesses. It was into this chaotic situation that Zhao Jing-yu arrived as the new executive director.

THINGS HAD BEEN going very smoothly in the army for Zhao—so smoothly in fact that he didn't see what was coming at him. He had risen to the rank of regimental commander in the People's Liberation Army, a position equal to departmental director in civilian administration. Zhao had always made it clear that he would accept without question any appointment from his superiors in the army or the Party. However, finding a suitable position for Zhao had recently become problematic for the army. Zhao was fifty-four and not well educated. It was definitely too late to enroll him in any kind of training program. Nowadays no military unit would welcome an uneducated person of fifty-four. In broaching the subject of transfer to civilian work, the division commander put it this way: "Look, Old Zhao, the fact is,you're never going to get promoted anymore as long as you stay in the army, not even one more rank. You see what I'm getting at?" Zhao saw and understood, to his sorrow. But he knew there was no use in self-pity, so he bucked up, and said, "I will submit a request for transfer to civilian work." The division commander was moved by Zhao's good sense and promised to help him find a rewarding, new position.

During his first two years of civilian service, Zhao had passed through four work units. At the same time, Yao Chun-gang's wife was working as a temp in the Office of Staff Reduction. She knew that China Psychological History Research Institute was looking for an executive director and suggested that her office transfer Zhao Jing-yu there. The director of the office agreed and placed a phone call to the institute. Yao Chun-gang took the call while watching two coworkers play chess.

"Is this the Psychological Research Institute?"

Yao replied, "No. They're different. We're the China Psychological *History* Research Institute. We do the same thing they do, but we're two different units. If you're looking for them, this is the wrong number."

The caller hurried to say, "No, no—you're the ones I was trying to reach. Is your executive director's position vacant?"

"Yes, yes."

"Good. We should like to send you a new director, a man who is excellent in all respects! Would you welcome him?"

Yao replied, "Welcome him? Of course! We're waiting for a good director to come in and take control of this mess. Nobody's been willing to touch it so far."

"Then it's settled."

"Uh huh . . . We'll be expecting this 'excellent-in-all-respects' person to get over here as soon as possible."

Yao absently returned the receiver to its cradle and his full attention to the chess match. He had never asked which department the caller represented. Nor did the caller ask who Yao was at China Psychological History Research Institute. Yao had conducted the entire interview without ever taking his eyes off the chessboard.

When Yao got home after work, his wife asked him about the call. After a moment's reflection Yao said, "I'm the one who took it."

His wife scolded him. "Who do you think you are? How can you speak for the whole institute?"

He laughed and dismissed her concerns with a wave of his hand. "He'll only be a figurehead. We need somebody, all right, but none of us wants to be in charge. Everybody's bumbling around like a headless fly. Who knows what stupid things they could do without anyone in charge."

The next day at work, Yao mentioned the telephone conversation and nearly set off a riot. Staff members said it was completely absurd to give a soldier command over psychologists. "We're not some flock of sheep that anybody can drive along with a stick!" said one.

The day after that, Zhao Jing-yu arrived at China Psychological History Research Institute to take up his post. He rode in on an old bicycle with a brand-new briefcase strapped to the carriage rack. The aging security guard stopped him at the reception office and asked whom he might be looking for.

"I'm not looking for anybody. I'm here to be the new executive director."

"Nobody told me anything about it," the old guard muttered suspiciously.

"Well, I'm telling you now," Zhao said.

The guard still wouldn't let Zhao enter, thinking that the man on the bicycle could be some kind of nut. He telephoned office after office, trying to find someone who would come down to the reception room. Finally, all of the staff came down.

Zhao did not seem like a nut to the psychologists. They could read him well enough. They gathered round him, though the reception was chilly. In no time, the excitable ones let Zhao know that he was not welcome at the institute. Their calmer colleagues suggested he would be wise to get himself a more suitable situation somewhere else because the administrative psychologists were really going to stick it to him if he hung around there too long.

Zhao waited patiently: the model of self-restraint. He listened to each one of the comments quietly. After all the workers had said whatever it was they had to say and had run out of anything new to bring up, Zhao began to speak.

His words astonished them all. "Attention, each of you! Enough of the nonsense," he said. "I picked this place. I picked this street. I picked this little building. I'm not going anywhere. I am the executive director and will continue to be. You can't push me out. Don't act like psychology is so mysterious. I was a regiment commander for over ten years. I commanded a thousand disciplined, mindful, and obedient officers and soldiers. You think I don't know psychology? Well, Zhao Jing-yu doesn't go and swallow the sickle if his belly isn't curved to fit it! Here's the truth: If I don't discipline every one of you into a willing, obedient subordinate, then I didn't come from the family Zhao!"

Having said his piece, he walked boldly toward the building, leaving everyone else behind to stare in mute amazement.

Without anyone to show the way, Zhao located the executive director's office on the second floor. A small padlock sealed the entry. Troubling to obtain neither permission nor the key, he wrenched the door open with a single shoulder thrust and stepped in. This is how the new arrival inaugurated his tenure as executive director.

The curious ones who had followed him as far as the stairwell and watched from a defensive position below scowled and warned each other that this was somebody not to cross. Nobody dared go up to the second floor.

He stayed upstairs by himself the whole morning, putting his new office in order. The security guard watched from outside as Zhao wiped the windows until they shined.

Later in the morning, one of the young men tiptoed to the doorjamb to peek into the office. A moment later he scurried back downstairs, alerting office after office: "Now he's making phone calls!" A second scout reported, "Now he's reading a newspaper!" Understandably, given the quality of these reports, interest in the situation began to lag. Making phone calls and reading newspapers is what everybody did at the institute.

Later the old security guard carried a thermos of fresh, piping hot water upstairs to the boss. On his return he told everyone he met, "Looks like we have a leader who really wants to do something. That old office is spotless now. None of the other directors even came close."

The staff glared at him. He didn't have any trouble reading their minds: *Surrendering so quickly? Fetching him his hot water, are we? Already kissing up?*

"Well—he called me and told me to bring him some hot water! He's the new boss. I'm just a temp. Do I dare to disobey?"

The new director remained upstairs into the afternoon. A third scout sneaked upstairs on reconnaissance and discovered that the hallway had been mopped. The hallway window glass shined. No one had ever seen the hallway look so clean.

At quitting time the security guard stopped everybody at the reception room to tell them of the new director's decision: "Because it's been so hot, everyone gets two cases of canned orange drink. You can take them home with you. If anyone wants to keep some in their office, you'll get another case of it delivered to you tomorrow."

This caught everyone off guard. "How did he get all this stuff without going out of his office?" they wanted to know.

"He called a grocery store. They delivered it."

"I'll bet he doesn't know that the last director already gave us our three-month antiheat allowance," one employee speculated.

The security guard corrected him. "He knew. I told him we already got our antiheat money. But he said, 'None of my business. The last executive director gave them their antiheat allowance; can't I compensate for the extra-hot weather?'"

This caused the staff to ponder. Many heads turned and eyes looked upward at the shiny office window. Most, in their own way, asked themselves, *Why would we want to get rid of a director like him? We're lucky to have a director who cares about us.*

The first people to arrive at the institute the next morning found that the front court had been carefully swept. The perennials and ornamental shrubs that had struggled along both sides of the front steps for years in forlorn neglect were now watered, weeded, and expertly trimmed, so that even they exuded optimism. Upon entering the building, the early arrivals found that the ground-floor hallway and windows had been cleaned. No one had bothered to clean the hallway since the previous boss left weeks ago. Since nobody had actually seen the new director come downstairs to do any of this tidying up, the change seemed all the more miraculous. As more of the staff arrived and marveled, all wanted to go upstairs to say something appreciative, and they would have, except for a psychological obstacle: they were embarrassed.

At noon a buffet car loaded with box lunches, hot meat and vegetable dumplings, pickled vegetables, beer, and pastries pulled into the yard. The security guard informed all staff members that Director Zhao had arranged for lunch to be delivered, and that it would come every workday from now on. If anyone wanted something that didn't appear on the menu, talk to the driver. Further, everyone would be receiving a one-yuan subsidy toward each day's lunch. The old security guard had pointedly said "Director Zhao," as if the man had been there for twenty years. Zhao himself did not come down to buy his own lunch. The old guard selected some dishes, paid for them, and carried them up to the director's office. On his return he mentioned to those whom he passed along the way that Director Zhao was fixing the bathroom faucet on the second floor.

Yao Chun-gang took the opportunity during the lunch hour to pressure the employees into going up to the executive director's office. They hesitated, but they saw Yao's point. After lunch one by one they crept upstairs. Each apologized for his or her initial rudeness, laying the blame on the previous director's cold, bureaucratic style, and expressing their extreme admiration for Zhao Jing-yu.

Zhao Jing-yu smoked one cigarette after another and listened without interrupting. Every time he wanted another smoke, he took the pack out of his pocket, lit up, and immediately put the pack away as if he were afraid someone might snatch it up and run off with it. He never offered anyone else one of his smokes; never received any offers, either. He seemed indifferent to what was going on.

After the last had finished bad-mouthing the previous director and praising the incumbent, all expected Zhao Jing-yu to respond, probably to talk for quite a while. Instead he said, "I'll have more good news for you, but just stow your praises."

Part Two

"YOUNG YAO! WHAT'S wrong with your foot?" cried the old security guard the moment Yao Chun-gang got out of the car.

Yao's heart felt even heavier, not because of the old man's reaction, but because he had used the diminutive address. Not once since he had advanced to vice director had anyone in the institute addressed him as "Vice Director" or "Director Yao." But Zhao Jing-yu! Everybody addressed him as "Director Zhao" with respect; not a single one ever called him "Old Zhao," like you would a regular guy. This further encouraged Yao's suspicion that there was only one director in the employees' eyes. As far as anyone there was concerned, Yao was the assistant, plain and simple, a position which, filled or vacant, didn't make a bit of difference.

"*Ouch!* It's going to be a bad day. My athlete's foot flared up. Then it got infected," he explained, stifling his annoyance.

"Really? You're still coming to work?"

"How could I not? Old Zhao called me at home. Then he sent his car to pick me up. Would I dare stay home?"

Yao would have appreciated a little sympathy, even though technically his foot was not in any pain. Sympathy, though, was not to be had, and so he satisfied himself by implying to the security guard that Zhao Jing-yu was not all that considerate a person.

The security guard continued, "If he sent his car to pick you up, he must have something important to talk to you about. It's too bad it has to be so"—he groped for the word—"so inconvenient for you."

It was obvious that the man was on Zhao Jing-yu's side.

"Yeah, yeah," Yao muttered as he turned and walked away. "Who else is he going to talk to if I'm not here?" Yao had not liked the old security guard's words.

The guard called after him, "You sure you can get upstairs by yourself? Need any help?"

That refocused Yao's attention. He began to groan, lurching slowly on his "good" foot, barely touching the ground with the "bad" one. He suddenly recognized a novel opportunity.

"Yes, I guess I do need some help. I . . . I can't make it upstairs by myself."

The security guard moved quickly to help support him.

The sight of his assistant limping into his office with one arm slung across the shoulder of the guard startled Director Zhao. Staring wide-eyed at the bandaged foot, he stammered, "Oh! I didn't think . . . it was . . . Why didn't you tell me on the phone? I wouldn't have had you come in if I knew it was . . . this serious."

"No, no, please; it's boring to stay home," Yao said with a

confidential shrug. "I'd rather be here at work any day, especially when you need my help."

Zhao Jing-yu hurried to scoot an overstuffed chair up to Yao and insisted that he sit down. Then he carefully cradled Yao Chun-gang's "infected" left foot with both hands until it was settled safely on a soft ottoman.

"Are you sure you're doing the right thing . . . being here?" Zhao asked. "You know, you're making me feel guilty."

It seemed obvious to Yao that the executive director was trying to relieve his own conscience as much as he wanted to comfort his assistant.

Yao Chun-gang felt so pleased inside, especially from the moment when Zhao Jing-yu carefully supported his foot with both hands. The sensation of well-being coursed through his body as though an acupuncture needle had hit the main pleasure sensor. His whole body tingled, feeling weightless. Every tissue and joint felt revitalized. Yao was deeply touched—thirty percent in actuality and seventy percent for the benefit of Director Zhao.

Zhao Jing-yu poured a cup of green tea for him. He handed Yao a cigarette and lit it up; it was only one of his cheap Hiltons, but it was the first time Zhao Jing-yu had ever shared his cigarettes. Yao was surprised at how flattered he was feeling.

A female visitor of about thirty-four or thirty-five also was present in the director's office. The elegant, lavender dress she wore made it clear there would be no obesity in her future. Her bare, fair-skinned legs looked very long, and slanted smartly in parallel lines. Yao Chun-gang appreciated a woman who had long legs. Whatever the rest of her may look like, if the legs were long he would remember what eyes were made for.

When his eyes discovered this visitor, she did not avoid his gaze or appear embarrassed in any way. On the contrary, she basked in the attention like a patient undergoing sunlamp treatment. He thought her face resembled that of a rabbit. Her eyes were too far apart, and her nose too close to her lips. Such a face was a bit peculiar, but by no means a disgrace. She used cosmetics lightly and adeptly. He could see she knew what she was doing because she artfully brought her eyes closer together with the help of an eyebrow pencil. He also noticed how boldly she spoke with her eyes. Eloquent eyes can command one's attention sharply and silently—not to suggest that Yao Chun-gang's eyes had been entirely mute! By the time that Zhao Jing-yu got around to introducing the two, Yao and the woman had already conducted a very pleasant "conversation."

And who are you?

I am a woman.

I think I like you.

Lots of men like me.

Are you the giving sort?

Well, it all depends. What do you want from me?

Suppose I want all of you.

Depends on how you want it.

Zhao Jing-yu had been talking on the phone. It provided more than enough time for the man and woman to get to know each other. More than her eyes alone, her entire body bespoke a desire for intimacy. The desire, once confessed, seemed to ignite the woman's eyes, which, with the complicity of her refined reticence, had utterly seduced him. She fixed her gaze to announce quite unmistakably: *Be patient, my man. You'll have your hour.*

By this time Zhao Jing-yu was shouting over the phone. Yao Chun-gang didn't notice a word of it, so focused was he on the creature seated opposite him. After all was said and done, Yao was a gentleman, not a lecher. Perhaps a more accurate statement would be that he had never willingly delivered himself up to a seductress. Further, when it came to looks, Yao's wife had nothing to worry about from this rabbit-faced woman. Let us summarize here and say that a man's decency remains unestablished until it is tested by a capable woman.

Zhao Jing-yu hung up the phone and then politely introduced the woman to Yao Chun-gang. Her name was Qu Xiujuan; she had been a classmate of Zhao's niece. She presently owned a small shop that produced clothing and employed thirty girls. She was calling on Zhao to ask for his help and support because business had not been so good.

Zhao introduced Yao Chun-gang as "My assistant. He just took up the post."

Hearing himself presented in such a manner irritated Yao. He would never accept that a vice director could be properly thought of as an *assistant* to the executive director. Further, why in the world would anyone say something like "He just took up the post"? *Obviously*, thought Yao, *Zhao Jing-yu is cluing her in that I have no real power in the institute . . . that I'm some kind of lieutenant or shadow of Zhao Jing-yu.*

Yao acknowledged the introduction and purred, "Yes, I always listen to Director Zhao. I always follow his instructions." Though the comment was addressed to the woman, the timbre of his voice unmistakably attested to his modesty and loyalty to Zhao Jing-yu. He could see the old man loved it.

Zhao Jing-yu turned to Yao and said, "Young Yao, you take over from here. I want you to stand in for me and finish up with Young Comrade Qu. I'm out of time. Meeting some Hong Kong businessmen for breakfast." He glanced at his watch and muttered, "It's already too late for any damned breakfast."

The young woman blushed at the older man's crude

language. Noticing the uncertainty in her eyes, Yao Chun-gang began to sympathize with her. They both realized that Zhao had just written her off. She smiled up at Yao with a face still red from embarrassment and eyes that made her pitiable.

Zhao rose and patted Yao on the shoulder. "You handle it. I trust you." The unmistakable message in Zhao's eyes, however, was *Don't get yourself mixed up with this woman. Get rid of her as fast as you can.* It occurred to Yao that Zhao must have already become impatient with her before he arrived. That moved him to take even more pity on her. As soon as the door closed behind Zhao, their facial conversation resumed, except that now the gazing was unrestrained, aggressive though gentle, and intimate.

She said, "Your foot must be numb. Would you like to have it off the ottoman for a while?"

He felt comfortable the way it was, but said, "You're right. My whole leg is numb."

He yearned to get nearer to her, hungered to hold those delicate, red-nailed hands. She knew this.

The woman rose from her chair and gently picked up his leg with both hands. She was *cradling* his leg in her arms, not just supporting it. As she moved, his leg brushed the softest part of her body. *That soft spot must be pretty big,* he thought. The image that immediately sprang up in his mind jolted him so abruptly that he almost lost control of himself.

She nestled his foot on the floor. Then, instead of returning to her chair, she squatted down beside him like a dog at the foot of its master. She raised her eyes to discern his mood, much like a dog that has served its master faithfully and awaits the acknowledgment. Between master and pet it is a tender moment; replace the dog with a woman and the master is going to encounter considerably more than tender feelings. He looked at her. His gaze lingered upon the loosely opened neckline. He noticed something pink—the edge of her bra. He felt that what he was doing was shameful, even vile, but he could not rein in his eyes.

She asked in a low voice, "Is it very numb?"

He said, "Yeah, very."

He began to moan and complain. "Such hot weather. My leg is a mess. I had to come in just to please him," he said, referring to Zhao.

She said, "Just tell yourself the only reason you're doing this is *for me.* . . ." She looked up into his eyes affectionately from the corners of her own. He returned the sentiment with a restrained, expectant smile.

"I've studied massage. Want me to give you a leg massage? It'll help the blood circulate and make you feel all better." He nodded in assent but glanced meaningfully at the door. She rose, tiptoed to the door, and locked it.

She returned and sat down in the overstuffed chair opposite him. She drew up her skirt, raised his "numb" leg to her charming, exposed knees, and began to massage. She started at his ankle and worked her way gradually upward. Her fingers kneaded his skin with robust attention to detail, exactly the way a professional would do. With every advance up his leg, her body tilted forward until his bandaged foot pressed against her soft belly, itself almost as soft as the breast he had touched. He closed his eyes to indulge in a fantasy or two. Her hands worked up to and beyond his knee. Without a pause she continued massaging upward, and upward still, until coming to rest beyond the point where a reputable masseuse would stop. There she hesitated, rather like a snail that has come to a wall and must decide what to do next.

He opened his eyes and saw her gazing intently up at him.

Her self-confident face belied her uncertain hands. Oblivious to any uncertainty, though, what he saw was the inexorable determination of a woman who achieves her goals. She hadn't expected him to open his eyes. She quickly smiled, keeping her hands poised in place.

But the smile came too late. The picture of raw determination before him quickly dashed the pleasant scenario he had imagined. The eyes he glimpsed were those of a surgeon about to remove a tumor. Before proceeding, surgeon and patient have to negotiate an agreement. If he, as the patient, agrees, the operation will proceed to conclusion; if he does not, she will lay down her instruments. Of course, the tissue in question was tumescent, rather than tumorous.

He was overcome with humiliation. The excitement that had boiled his blood was nothing more than the product of his own wishful thinking. He felt like a cow waiting for the milk-maid; that was it for the excitement—waiting to be serviced by a pair of hands. What a joke!

That bitch! he cursed in his heart.

Shamed into anger he pushed her hands away. He yanked his leg from her knees and thrust it into the slipper he had worn to work.

For a moment she looked disconcerted, but she quickly regained her air of dignity. She rose and moved to the place where she had been sitting when Yao Chun-gang arrived. Standing in a graceful pose with one hand's fingers touching the back of the sofa, she asked, "Is it still numb?"

"No. Much better," he said.

She gave him a canny smile.

The figure she presented would be the envy of any thirty-five-year-old woman. Her arms and legs were long, her breasts high, and the waist very slim—not anorexic, but salubrious, lithe. Her neck was her best feature in this pose: the parallel grooves along her throat ranked with haute-couture models sauntering down a Shen Zhen runway. Her lips became still fuller and decidedly more crimson as she moistened them with her tongue. She evoked the image of a proficient lounge waitress who is forced to deal with a surly but important customer: she watches out for herself while being polite and keeping the customer happy. This confused Yao. He couldn't decide whether his wicked thoughts had driven her away or her pretensions of innocence had brought this embarrassment on him. She looked like a decent woman, so decent and natural that it was hard to believe it could all be a lie. Anyway, now he felt really embarrassed. He pointed to the door. She stepped over and unlocked it.

He said, "Would you mind opening the door? It would let some fresh air in."

She opened the door wide. A sudden gust blew a few sheets of paper off the desk. She stooped into a graceful pose to pick them up. One sheet had landed by his bandaged foot. Rather than move her body closer to him, she stretched toward him to retrieve the paper. She did this while keeping her eyes on him, ready to withdraw her arm in an instant if he should sweep her up in an embrace and ravish her.

Now he was totally puzzled. He picked up the paper and handed it to her. She took it, put it on the desk together with the others she had picked up, and anchored the sheets with a porcelain pencil jar. Then she moved the overstuffed chair they had been using back to its original position and sat down at the precise place where she had sat originally.

"Thanks for the massage," he said.

"I do hope it helps," she said quite sincerely.

"Where did you learn how to do massages?"

"I used to have a beauty salon. I read up on it whenever I had time. Gradually it became another service I could offer my customers."

"So, you're a self-educated expert."

"It's easy. Anybody who wants to learn how can pick it up really fast."

"Then why did you go into producing clothing?"

"Because of men like you."

"What do you mean?"

She stopped talking and let her eyes respond: *You know perfectly well what I mean.*

Now his foot had gone to sleep. What else could he expect—the bandage was wound around it so tight. He wondered if it would be better to put it back up on the ottoman. He felt the numbness spreading up through his whole leg. He wondered what she would say if he asked her to massage his leg again. Would she refuse? As he looked at her, mulling over his uncertainties, the autonomous impulses began to assert themselves again.

"Would you close the door?" he said.

She got up to close the door. With her hand detained on the bolt, she fixed her eyes on him with a look of absolute obedience. The message was unmistakable—a definitive nod from him and she would lock it. He found himself admiring her shrewdness, for it appeared that she had seen right through him, but he immediately dismissed that idea with a laugh. She had only detected a single thought passing through his mind, nothing more. She could never know what he really thought about women. Although Yao had never gotten involved with any woman other than his wife, the inclination to do so had always existed. He had always restrained such impulses. Sometimes the restraint required serious effort, so much so that he could find himself at the very threshold of delirium. There he would be, discussing the soberest matter with a woman while imagining himself in a bedded frenzy with her—if she turned him on. Of course, the woman he was talking to had no idea any of this was occurring. Women regarded him as a serious man. It would be more accurate to call him a cautious man. Yao did not behave rashly because he was too distrustful and unenterprising. Today, though, Yao was neither. The present circumstances had rendered caution unnecessary. Executive Director Zhao Jing-yu's car was not standing in the yard, so there was no reason for anybody to come looking for him upstairs. All the other offices had been moved downstairs in accordance with Zhao Jing-yu's decision to rent out the unused second-floor office spaces for additional income. Therefore, the hour and conditions were perfect for Yao to crawl out of his cocoon of self-restraint. He nevertheless analyzed the situation one more time: *Is there anything that could possibly go wrong? No, nothing to worry about. There is even a bed in the back room, the one Zhao Jing-yu uses for his cat-naps after lunch. The bed is clean and solid, which is important because a creaking bed would distract from the pleasure.* The last remaining concern was one of Yao's personal quirks. He did not like—or at least wasn't used to—women who gave in just like that. He understood that she was sacrificing her honor to attain her own ends. Yao could not accept a sacrifice made to him until he knew for certain what her goal was and whether he was even in position to help her attain it. Yao was one who always played by the rules—because when the game was over, he wanted to come out owing nothing to anyone. At this point he shook his head at her to say no.

She withdrew her hand from its position on the bolt.

"Would you sit down?"

She complied but took time to refill his tea mug with hot water as a way to attenuate the awkwardness of the situation.

"Let's talk," he said.

She began to speak softly: "Hasn't Director Zhao ever mentioned my case to you?"

"No, he hasn't."

"I've come to see him several times. Each time he's told me he'll have to discuss things with you."

"He's never said a word about you to me."

"Then . . . then he's evading me."

"Oh, don't look at it like that. He's a busy man."

"Are you the one that . . . who can make certain decisions?"

He shrugged.

She wanted to get to the point but hesitated.

Yao lit up a cigarette, waiting patiently for her to get her words out.

She pulled herself together and continued. "Director Zhao said you had been one of the 'educated youth' sent to the countryside."

"That's true."

"One of the city kids sent to the Great Northern Wasteland?"

"Yes."

"Were you with the Production Corps or on a farm?"

"The corps."

"Me, too."

"You?"

"We have similar backgrounds."

She smiled at him to suggest that they shared a special relationship, and the thought of it fascinated him. Yao reflected that if she had claimed such a thing outright, he might have thought her vulgar or even manipulative. *She knows very well when to withhold speech, the importance of unspoken lines. She understands there are times when a woman's smile says more than any spoken language,* he reasoned.

"Which division were you in?"

"Second."

This information subtly shifted the situation. Yao began to probe. "Which regiment?"

"Ninth."

"We were in the same regiment."

"Really?"

"Sure. What company were you in?"

"Sixth," she answered.

"I was in the Seventh."

"I was almost assigned to the Seventh Company!" She looked at him with a gaze of deep intimacy, suggesting what a disappointment it was that she had not been assigned to his company. She added, "I felt really let down when I couldn't get assigned to the Seventh."

He suddenly realized that she was massaging him with her eyes instead of her hands. The sensation persisted. "Why couldn't you get assigned to Seventh Company?" He was feeling sorry for her himself.

"What else could it be?"

"You were the daughter of a capitalist leader?"

She shook her head. He felt stupid to have made such a blunder. Her family background would not affect her assignment to any particular company. Their eyes met again, this time embracing inextricably before melting together.

"Then why on earth couldn't you get assigned to Seventh?"

"Because they heard I was having an affair with another high-school student, and they wanted to separate us." She smiled again more brilliantly than before.

"And the truth is . . ."

Yao Chun-gang relished hearing others retell their stories of past loves. He himself had never experienced the joys of romance during his bachelorhood. Yao's parents forbade him to have a girlfriend throughout his corps service, fearing that their son might never be able to return from his education through work in the countryside. For the entire seven years the man heeded his parents' words and avoided love like a pestilence. The girls thought he must have either a physical defect or a mental one. It didn't bother him. Actually, it spared him a lot of trouble. He never became entangled in any kind of dispute over sexual misconduct or harassment. In 1977 Yao returned to the city without a problem. He considered himself one of the luckiest people of the decade and his parents to be among the most sagacious. By 1979 almost all "educated youth" had returned to their families in the cities—including the ones who had married, and even those who had married local farmers. It was then that misgivings began to creep into Yao's psyche. Compared with most young people of his day, he had suffered a great loss: he had not loved, had not experienced love in the flower of his youth. It didn't matter that he was by then married. Marriage could not soothe his sense of loss. Indeed, it was his marriage that deprived him of making up for the lost romance that should rightfully have been his. He believed there ought to be compensation for his loss, even if only on a symbolic level. One way Yao found to compensate was to listen to former "educated youth" reminisce about their flings out in the countryside. He sought out similar personal accounts in the newspapers and magazines, not giving much thought as to whether the stories were verifiable. Yao was especially fond of love stories that were painful, sentimental, and which concluded in misery. But rather than feel sympathy for the heroes and heroines of his age, he was jealous of them. The more the narrators choked with sobs, the more jealous he grew. It was that way with anything he read about romance.

So he was hopeful she would tell a long, miserable story filled with complications; at the very least, it should be sentimental and melancholic. It must be about herself, too, of course. He had plenty of time today. He would demonstrate what a good listener he was. Yao even resolved that if she told a satisfying story, he would help her with her business. He would even do the seducing, instead of surrendering to her on the bed in Old Zhao's office. That would spare her those tedious little ploys.

"And the truth is? . . ." He prompted again.

"That is the truth," she whispered.

"How so?"

"We were having an affair."

"And then?"

"Then he fell for another girl . . . in Ninth Company, a Shanghai girl . . ."

This buoyed his spirits. He leaned forward, fully persuaded that a long, miserable story filled with complications was unfolding.

She continued. "Then I was in love with another young man, a Tianjin boy."

"Right away?"

She squinted at him, momentarily thrown off.

"I mean . . . did the first boyfriend fall in love with the Shanghai girl right away?"

"Yes. Less than a month after we separated."

"I see. And you?"

"I was in love with the Tianjin boy within ten days after the first one left me."

"Were you doing this to get even?"

"Kind of, but not totally. The Tianjin boy was actually more handsome. I was attracted to him right away, and I caught his eye at the same time. We saw each other secretly. No one ever knew. Once, a bit later, I ran into my first lover again, over in Ninth Company. I asked him if he didn't think he owed me something. He said, 'Yeah, I do.' We were on a country road. He grabbed my hand and pulled me toward the woods."

"So, you were reluctant, then—pretty much?"

"I don't know. Thirty percent reluctant, seventy percent willing—something like that. In the woods we—"

"You made love."

She laughed.

And so did he.

"In eleven years as an 'educated youth,' I loved over twenty times. Twice a year on average. My superiors criticized me for fooling around. But after my public criticism sessions, more young men showed up to take advantage of me. My eleven years were not completely wasted. I protected everyone who had an affair with me. The company higher-ups told me to write down their names. I didn't betray anyone, except the ones the company already knew about. The other ones, who had kept our meetings secret, showed their appreciation."

She paused for a moment before resuming.

"But I suffered, too. I had two abortions. After all these years, I can still count every one of my loves one by one. I've been true to myself, too."

"True to your values?"

"Yes, my values. I think I'm living a pretty good life. It's not worse than the way a lot of other people are living. I run my own business—a small garment workshop with over thirty girls. It's a living, at least. It hasn't been easy for me, either. A lot of my men friends have helped me. I never forget them, either. I repay their kindness. I give to those who are fond of me whatever a woman can give a man. . . . Don't look at me like that! What's there to act surprised about? I take a man-woman relationship at face value, just like anything else. There's nothing compared to what a woman can do if she's completely on her own. I even give money to men. I give out more to the ones who are close to me. Money means nothing to me. I make a lot of money and I spend it. I don't have any psychological snags, either. I'm divorced. Single. My husband agreed to a divorce after I bought him off. I am absolutely a liberated woman. The one I sleep with is my decision and nobody else's! You know, I never cause problems for their families, either. Some of my men's wives are my closest friends. When I get in trouble, the wives run all over town to help me out. Why? For one thing, they know I'll never take their husbands away from them. What would I want their husbands for—to marry me? I do not need a husband! I would get bored spending day after day with the same man. What I do is comfort these ladies' husbands for them. Show me a man nowadays that doesn't need to have some tender, loving comfort. Sometimes the wives just don't know how to comfort them, but it wouldn't make any difference if they did know how. I know you men very well: what you all need every once in a while is tender, loving comfort from some woman besides your wife. That is what I am quite able to provide. I'm really good. And," she said, leaning forward on the sofa, "I give away money. *That's* something other women don't do. You know, it's pretty difficult for women to be as generous as me. Sometimes when a husband and wife are quarreling and I hear about it, I go and see them. The first thing I ask the wife is, 'Is it over money? Oh, you say it isn't?' I still give them some money—to the wife, of course. Then I bring the husband to my place for a few days. I soothe him, comfort him. Because I soothe them down, they listen to me. After a few days, I return a happy husband to his wife. How could his wife not fall down with her head to the floor and thank me? What a good thing money is! When everyone has money, the country is peaceful; families are peaceful. I am actually the unseen interior support of a lot of 'stable families.' Family rifts are closed and healed by what I do. Most important of all, I am completely harmless to the men that have been intimate with me. They only gain from me. They never lose anything. I have never asked anyone to belong to me. Well, you asked me what my values are, and now you know. Don't you think the principles I live by are things most men can only dream of?"

She talked volubly and vivaciously. Her knees separated as she slowly cooled herself with the edge of her skirt. At this point Yao's gaze drifted downward from her face.

"Well?"

"What?" He raised his head sluggishly.

"My values: what do you think about them?"

"The . . . I . . ."

Her eyes brimmed with seduction. She shook her head as if to show her waning patience.

"Could you help me stand up?" he asked. He still had not forgotten about his "infected" foot. He had ordered himself to keep up the act come what may. His eyes, however, spoke otherwise.

She left her cushioned seat slowly and walked to the office door.

He heard the dead bolt click into place.

"No, I . . . I don't . . ."

She came up to him with a sweet smile and offered her arm for support.

"I don't mean to . . ."

They both murmured something brief. While one hand clasped her far shoulder, his nearer hand articulated his desires.

"Be patient," she whispered.

Neither could have said with certainty whether she walked him, or he led her, to the inner room.

THE FIRST THING Yao Chun-gang did when he got home to soak his foot in a basin of cold water. After having been bound up for six or seven hours, it really was starting to ache.

He immersed his foot in the water and groaned.

"What is it?" his wife asked, turning away from the immediate task of retracing her eyebrows.

"Nothing."

He groaned a bit more.

"Are you sure?"

"Yeah."

"Then why are you moaning?"

"It just . . . feels so good."

Indeed, the soothing comfort that flooded his entire body was difficult to describe. Fortunately for himself, Yao reflected, he was a thinking man, and thus able to recognize this novel truth: a guy makes his own fun. As long as he keeps his brain set on *creative*, he can enjoy all kinds of pleasures every day. The episode with the allegedly diseased foot led Yao Chun-gang to an even deeper truth: If he starved himself by skipping a few meals, how much more would he relish devouring the next meal. If he denied himself water for a whole day, he would then love gulping glassfuls like a fish. Let the mosquito go ahead and bite awhile; how soothing it would feel to scratch the itch. He could win the pleasure of exquisitely good sleep simply by cultivating insomnia through worry to distraction. He could . . .

His gaze rested on his wife. She had returned to her makeup. She was already wearing the eight hundred yuan outfit that they had saved for three months to buy. She was still a woman who could turn a man's head, even though her performance when she finally did get into bed was less than dazzling. She blamed him for the bedtime deficiencies, calling their lovemaking a miniseries in thirty-second episodes. She made him try herbal tonics, then sent him to a doctor—a friend with connections was able to get him in to see a specialist. The diagnosis was, "It's not the equipment." From that Yao concluded the problem must be psychological. So if he fasted sexually right up to the point of starvation, wouldn't it boost his performance in the sack? Then he would surely be able to satisfy his wife, wouldn't he? This line of thinking led him to yet another discovery—that failing to satisfy himself or others can be the result of too little "*If . . .*" thinking.

His wife turned to him again. "Oh, I'll be getting back late tonight." Her scrupulous application of makeup, enhanced with the virtues of the expensive dress, made her look elegant and charming, and at least ten years younger.

"Where are you going?"

"My job transfer came through today. I'm going out with some friends to celebrate." Her words were cool and studied.

"You changed your job? Why didn't you consult with me first, before you—"

"I did," she said peremptorily.

He searched his memory. Yes, technically she had consulted with him.

"But you only mentioned it once, and—"

"One time or a hundred, what does it matter? You never really care about my work."

She appraised her lipstick in the compact mirror: a bit too thick. She made adjustments with a handkerchief.

He watched as if he were looking at a stranger, thinking to himself, *Well, yes, I have cared about her work, haven't I?*

"There's some *jiaozi* in the freezer."

"I don't like frozen *jiaozi*. It ruins the taste."

"Also, there're some leftover doughnuts and *congee* you didn't finish at breakfast."

"You know I never have *congee* for dinner."

"Don't eat it, then. Just eat the doughnuts. But you'll have to dip the leftover *congee* out of the pot and put whatever you don't eat in the refrigerator."

"Where were you transferred?"

"Over to Jiatong."

"What kind of a company is that?"

"A trading company."

"What kind of trading?"

"They deal in everything except narcotics and human beings. Right now we're helping Russians get a MiG-31 and some missiles—"

"Missiles? . . ."

"Yes. Missiles. How come all of a sudden you're so interested in my job?"

"I'm just curious about it, that's all. Is it secret stuff?"

"No. It's—"

Short beeps from a car's horn outside interrupted her.

"Excuse me. They're here." She swung the little purse with the long strap over her shoulder and hurried away.

"Hey, wait! What's your new job?"

"Manager's assistant for public relations."

"Is that your boss's car?" he asked very pointedly.

"Yes," she answered, equally to the point.

The car's horn sounded again, even more insistently.

He waved his hand as if to dismiss her.

"If I'm not home by eleven o'clock, I'll probably be out all night."

As soon as his wife shut the front door, Yao fiercely threw the basin out of his way and rushed barefoot to the window. Hiding behind the drapery, he peered outside.

A man of about thirty-two or -three, handsome and well dressed, smirked as he opened the sedan's rear door for Yao's wife. Yao was not certain whether the man was his wife's boss, though he obviously was not the driver because another man sat at the wheel. The scene itself was suspicious enough, but his wife's behavior outside made it even more so. She had to have heard the basin hitting the floor; and she was smart enough to understand that she had walked out on an unsettled situation. As if that were not troubling enough, Yao plainly saw her repay the man's smirk with her own cheerful smile. She had spoken of a few friends going out to celebrate; what Yao was seeing was her boss or his assistant picking her up in a chauffeured car.

The spilled water caught up with him at the window and wet his bare feet. Stomping in the water seemed to help him vent his wrath. Of course, technically, he was punishing his feet rather than his wife, and he was making a mess. After his tantrum subsided, he sat on the sofa for a moment, still slowly seething, then went to the refrigerator and ate the breakfast leftovers. Without washing his greasy hands, he picked up the phone and dialed Zhao Jing-yu's number.

Zhao Jing-yu's wife answered. Zhao was not at home, hadn't been home for a few days, and may not get back today, either. She suggested that Yao call Zhao's office.

He called Zhao's office. The telephone rang for quite a while. Just as Yao was about to hang up, someone answered.

"Hello?" It was a young woman's voice.

"Hunh? Who are you?" he exclaimed.

The phone immediately went dead.

He stood dumbfounded for a moment then dialed the number again. This time no one picked up the receiver.

"Damn!"

Still feeling hungry, he went back to the kitchen and ladled out a full bowl of cold, watery *congee*. However, he abruptly stopped short of eating, and thought to himself, *No, not yet. Wait until you're starving.* He would attain the intense satisfaction he had mused about earlier.

When he returned to the living room, he was still wondering, *Who could that have been at Zhao's office?* The young woman's voice sounded familiar, even if he had heard only one word. As he searched his memory, the touched-up, pretty face of a young lady appeared. It was Xiao Zhang at the institute. She was a college graduate who had gotten assigned there after Zhao Jing-yu became executive director. She had come from a suburban county in Shanghai Prefecture and spoke with a Shanghai accent. He glanced at his watch. It was already past seven. He had been one of the last people remaining at the institute when he got away at four-thirty. If that had been the Shanghainese woman on the phone, what was she doing there so late? And in the executive director's office? Who gave her the key? Could she have gotten in without a key? No! Fat Zhao must be in the office, too. He recalled the scene that morning when he was in the executive director's office with the rabbit-faced massage therapist, and he was pretty sure that something along those same lines was going on there now.

Yao picked up the phone again.

This time the call was answered at the first ring. It was the executive director, Fat Zhao, himself. "Is this Young Yao?" he asked.

"Yes. I've been calling you."

"Oh . . . I just got back."

Liar! thought Yao.

"Well, Young Yao . . . what's up?"

"This morning at the office, that woman named Qu was in a rush to get an answer."

"Answer to what, eh?"

"About her using our institute's name to open a business—"

"No! Out of the question." Zhao Jing-yu cut him off before he could finish.

"She said it's just our name that she wants to use. She'll pay the administrative fee. She can even pay three years' fees in advance, and—"

"Don't even think about it."

"Old Zhao, couldn't you just give it a little more thought?"

"There's nothing to think about. We're going to be starting up our own business."

"We are? You never told me about this."

"It's not too late to tell you now."

"Well . . . What shall I say to Miss Qu, then?"

"Tell her straight out what I'm telling you! This morning when I was leaving, I tapped you on the shoulder deliberately. Didn't you understand what I meant?"

Yao lied, mumbling that he hadn't understood.

"Did you promise her something?"

"No, no—not without getting your approval. You must know that I would never decide anything on my own."

There was another lie. He had already made significant promises. Not in Zhao Jing-yu's bed, of course; not even in that room. Where he had indeed made his promises was at the gate of the institute as he walked her to the street and shook her hand. He told her that her proposition was no problem at all; just wait for the good news. He assured her that even if Zhao Jing-yu was unhappy with the idea, the old man wouldn't turn it down completely. Besides, up to then Yao had never disagreed with any of Zhao's decisions, so it was high time for Zhao to go along with one of Yao Chun-gang's plans. Yao also had promised Qu he would phone her the good news by eight o'clock that evening.

"Old Zhao, let's look at this from her perspective: she's all set to hear good news, but now we have to tell her to put every-thing on hold?"

"All set for good news? I never promised her anything. You didn't, either. How'd she get her hopes up?"

"Well, I . . . I mean, it's—"

"What are you trying to say?"

"Well, what I'm trying to say is . . . 'Let him who tied the belt on the tiger take it off.' It would be much better if you phoned her the news."

"What do you mean—'tied the belt'! I didn't tie any damn belt on anything, so I don't need to untie it! Yao Chun-gang . . . are *you* tied up with this woman?"

"No. No. What are you talking about? Of course I'm not. How could any woman wrap me up so easily?"

He waited for Zhao Jing-yu to stop laughing. After a moment Zhao continued, now speaking authoritatively.

"You must know how busy I am, day in and day out, day

after day. Can't you handle a trifling matter like this by yourself? As my assistant, you should be taking my responsibilities into consideration."

Yao could not fail to hear the dissatisfaction, the criticism, and most of all the accusatory tone in Zhao's words. "Chun-gang," Zhao said pointedly, "they named you 'steel' for a reason. Show some strength! And don't ever forget that *you* are *my* assistant! I never want to see that woman again. I don't want to hear her name. I don't even—"

"My name 'gang' is *not* the character for 'steel'!" Yao shouted, and slammed the receiver down on its cradle.

Assistant! Always his assistant! fumed Yao. *Well, I happen to be the assistant* director! He wanted to roar out his rage.

The telephone rang. Yao stared at it motionlessly. It continued to ring, but he could not summon the mettle to pick up the receiver. He looked at his watch. The time was five past eight. It could only be Qu. Her bribe had been to give her body to him. He had accepted her bribe but now was unable to deliver his end of the bargain. The situation looked more and more worrisome. What if she started coming to his office every day and went around saying things to people? What if she came to his home? Suppose she refused to just get over it? What would he do? She could even destroy him, if she chose to.

The telephone continued to ring. The jangling sound ravaged his nerves as if it were a snarling mastiff about to pounce.

Yao ran into the bedroom and grabbed a blanket to smother the telephone's ringing. This muted the sound but did not silence it. What's worse, the softened ringing grated on his eardrums even more, as if the ringing was now coming from somewhere inside his mind. Yao fled to the bed and stretched out with a pillow and crammed it over both ears. The telephone rang on, outside and inside his head.

When it finally stopped, the pillow stayed locked tightly in place for a long while. As he lay there, Yao began to think about the man who always thought of him as his assistant.

He recalled his decision to accept the appointment to assistant director. Had he acted wisely or unwisely? At first he was pleased to have the extra fifty yuan added to his monthly pay. But now here he was, getting paid all of fifty yuan to be Fat Zhao's *assistant*! Did he ever sell himself cheap! At first Zhao Jing-yu had been rather nice and friendly, even close to him. He had even once said privately, "Young Yao, I know how I got my position here. Everyone needs a 'parcel of land under their feet' in this society. With a parcel of land, life is meaningful. Without it, life holds no interest. Look at the old comrades: Some are getting more energetic as they get older. Some get gloomy and depressed—they don't live long after they retire. Why? Because some people are able to hold on to their 'parcel of land,' while others lose everything. This institute is *our* parcel of land. I got you promoted to repay you and your wife for your kindness. You're younger than me. Someday, when I retire, this executive director's job will be yours. I'll be your adviser. I know, nowadays people don't like the idea of having a retiree come in to tell them how to run things. But if you said you needed me, who would say anything about it? You wouldn't kick me out on my own, would you?"

Of course Yao Chun-gang swore he would never do such a thing.

Zhao Jing-yu was nine years older than Yao Chun-gang. The mandatory retirement age was sixty, and Zhao had six more years to go. Yao would be fifty-one then, and he would have nine years to serve as executive director in his own right. He had never considered Zhao's parcel-of-land theory before. Zhao Jing-yu had opened up his eyes and helped him see the importance of having that bit of land. He had felt very grateful to Zhao and thought of him as his mentor. Yao was not an excessively ambitious man. The China Psychological History Research Institute was big enough for him. He was not particularly concerned about its nebulous status. If a plot of land was so important, the institute would be better than nothing. Further, anything could happen in six years. Looking on the bright side, it was not out of the question that Zhao would turn over to him a successful, distinguished institute after six years. He really had remained loyal to Zhao for quite a while, trying his best to be a good assistant. He took on tasks that Zhao was reluctant to do—and not just the odds and ends, either, but some of the riskier assignments where somebody significant was sure to get upset. Every work unit had someone like that. No matter how much they gave day after day, no one appreciated it, least of all the ones who always got out of the unpopular assignments. To make matters worse, such work was endless. If someone were to ask Yao about his main achievements as assistant director, there would not be much to say. Instead of significant achievements, there was quite a list of people that Yao had managed to offend. He had gotten along well with his colleagues before his promotion. Yet the cost of the little piece of land promised by Zhao had been the companionship of his coworkers. He came to terms with his new position by telling himself that he was doing it all for Fat Zhao, as if Yao's achievements could be measured by the number of people he had offended.

One day Yao noticed a draft of a planning document that had been prepared for the director's office. He told the typist that he was on his way to a meeting with the director and might as well take it along with him. To Yao's surprise the typist said she had to take it to the director herself. Yao asked why. She told him it was confidential. Yao laughed, saying that although it may be confidential to others, it definitely was not to him. The typist was adamant. She said the director's orders were that nobody else must see it except herself. Such a challenge to his status as the number-two decision maker was completely unacceptable to Yao. He informed the typist that he himself would deliver the planning papers to Director Zhao, and he walked away with them over her objections.

As Yao walked he looked into the envelope. What he saw stopped him short. It was a nine-year development plan broken down in three-year stages. Zhao Jing-yu had titled it "A 3-by-3 Project." The plan envisioned considerable increases in receipts, sourced both domestically and overseas, during each three-year stage. It described a psychological counseling clinic, a psychiatric hospital, a freestanding college of psychology, a journal of psychological research, a list of publications, instructional videos to be produced, a one-hundred-episode television series dealing with psychological issues, an international symposium on issues in human psychology. . . . As described in the plan, the institute could well become the largest psychological research center in China—maybe even in Asia! It could become the fountainhead of Asian psychology, exactly the way that Hollywood is the fountainhead of American movies. Yao had not expected Zhao Jing-yu to be so ambitious. This plan was certainly more promising than the parcel of land Zhao had talked about for retirement. Parcel? It was a whole realm! *Well, now, this is really something,* thought Yao. *This big tree he's growing will cast a good shade for me, too.* Yao decided to devote his best efforts to assisting Zhao with this plan. Some things puzzled him, though. Why hadn't Fat Zhao ever mentioned any of this to him? Wasn't this a mission for both of them? If the old man was going to retire in six years, why did this project stretch over nine years?

When he handed the pages to his superior, Zhao Jing-yu asked, "Did you read it?"

"No," Yao replied. "Do I need to?"

"No, you don't," Zhao replied indifferently. He put the pages into his desk drawer and locked it. "It's nothing but some general statistical figures."

"What kind of statistics this time?"

"For allocating this year's bonus. I can't be dumping every little odd job on you, can I?" There was a hint of apology in Zhao's voice. He immediately moved on to another subject.

A few days later, the typist disappeared from the institute. Yao asked around and learned that the woman had been fired.

A few more days passed, and he discovered a shining bronze plaque posted prominently on the front gate. It read PSYCHOLOGICAL RESEARCH MAGAZINE, INC. People told him that Xiao Zhang, the Shanghai girl who had taken his call in the director's office, had been named vice president and deputy editor in chief; needless to say, Zhao Jing-yu was the president and editor in chief. A surge of jealousy welled up in Yao. It was bad enough to hear the news from his colleagues instead of from Zhao Jing-yu himself; but it was an outrage to learn that the vice-president and deputy-editor-in-chief titles had not been awarded to him. However, his reply to the colleagues was a cool smile and an aside that Old Zhao must know what he's doing, and this actually was an excellent way to help the younger employees mature within the administrative structure.

From that day on, Yao lived in a state of unrelieved crisis, ever uncertain about his actual status in Zhao Jing-yu's eyes. Could the future not be as bright as he had thought? He thought about the development plans he had perused on the way to Zhao's office and began to wonder if there was any room in them for him—maybe not: maybe nothing at all, and he was being cheated. That kind of cheating was going on everywhere. He continued to hope that Zhao Jing-yu would find the proper moment to confide to him, perhaps with words something like, "Oh, and Chun-gang: I haven't had a chance to talk with you about Young Zhang's promotion. I hope I haven't caused any misunderstanding." If Zhao were to say something like that, Yao could get over the idea that he had been cheated.

This line of thinking calmed him. Yao really didn't need to have a large realm, not now and not in the future. A small plot of land along the lines that Zhao Jing-yu had described would be good enough. It must be exhausting to be the ruler of a large realm. Well, just this one episode at the institute had left him exhausted. Yao understood that he was not one of those ambitious, struggling climbers. What he wanted was a life free of anxiety. So long as Zhao kept a position open for him at the institute, what else should he really care about? Let Zhao himself rule. Yao wouldn't even care if Zhao replaced him with somebody else. At least he would still have some decent position somewhere for which he was qualified and deserving. After all, he had worked hard in assisting Zhao.

Still, there were those other issues. Zhao hadn't confided in him about the new bronze plaque going up on the front gate. Zhao hadn't informed him of Xiao Zhang's promotion. His jealousy returned and began to ferment into hatred. He hadn't ever questioned any of Zhao Jing-yu's decisions for risk of falling out with the director. Zhao had taken absolute control over the institute. People accepted it because of the benefits he provided for them. To fall out of favor with such a person could cost Yao his position as assistant. He would become a nobody or, worst of all, be driven out of the institute entirely.

Yao carefully buried his anger deep inside and summoned up his submissive, respectful attitude. He knew he was not a great actor overall but thought he had perfected this particular performance. Having completed this shift in his thinking, Yao began to regret hanging up on Fat Zhao. It was the first time he had ever gone out of control—and all on account of the rabbit-faced woman. Had he really gone too far, or not? He recalled the look of her skin. The exposed areas had tanned lightly, but the other places were so white and delicate that the memory of the moment of discovery again overwhelmed him. In reverie he saw himself engaged in a clandestine love affair with an aristocrat. His blood boiled anew each time his memory touched upon the love he had devoured so hungrily. Inevitably he also remembered the promises he had made to her in appreciation. But that damned Zhao Jing-yu was making it impossible to honor his promises. Yao had never intended to take advantage of her. Now, even if she did not confront him about this, he would be feeling guilty for a long time.

Yao became aware of the sound of someone knocking at the door. He got up and answered it. The neighbor's kid stood there.

"Oh, you *are* at home." The boy seemed surprised.

That comment in turn surprised Yao. "Yes, I've been home since I got back from work."

"Then why didn't you answer the phone when your wife called?"

"She called here?"

"She said she tried to call for a long time. First the line was busy, then nobody answered. She had to call us to tell you she won't be home tonight."

"Won't be home? Where's she going to be?"

"She didn't say. Just to let you know you don't need to wait up for her. Oh—also, she's going to go straight to work tomorrow morning."

"Oh, I see. I see. Thanks a lot. There must be a problem with the telephone connection. I need to get it fixed. . . ."

The boy asked about the phone problem, but Yao said something to put him off and closed the door. He stood motionless in the living room for a while. Suddenly he wanted to laugh. Everything that had happened since morning had been so absurd that he would be an idiot to take it seriously. Worry, aggravation, guilt—they were nothing but a complete waste of time. It suddenly occurred to Yao how easily he had faked out the boy. So then, he could fake out the rabbit-faced woman, too, couldn't he? Fat Zhao was fooling around with Xiao Zhang in his office, and hadn't he faked Yao out with just one word over the phone? His wife was probably offering herself to her boss for the night; in the morning she'd have to think up some excuse to fake out Yao. Wasn't it such fun to fake people out! Putting the question to himself that way made him want to laugh all the more. Yao resisted until he could not contain himself any longer. He burst into uproarious laughter. It was a beautiful experience, this palliative laughing.

The telephone rang again. Supposing it to be his wife still trying to get through, Yao rushed to the living room without a second thought and picked up the receiver.

"Chun gang? It's Jing-yu."

"Oh! . . . Hi . . . What's up?"

"I want to know why you lost your temper with me awhile ago."

"I didn't do that—did I?"

"No? Then why did you bang the receiver down when I was talking?"

"I . . . knew that was the way it must have seemed to you. I've developed this kind of bony growth on my cervical vertebra . . . in my neck. My whole arm goes numb. Can't hold on to anything tight. I really need to take a few days off and go see a doctor."

"Oh, I see. Your foot still isn't well enough to walk on, either, is it? Anytime you need a car, just give me a call."

"Thank you so much, but that car's specially designated for you to use. What if you needed it?"

"Oh yeah, you're right. I have been pretty busy these days. Wouldn't make it without a car. Well, you can take a cab. I'll reimburse you."

"That's . . . You don't need to do that. Thanks, anyway. I appreciate it."

"You're welcome. Say, um, I was noticing my bedsheet today, and it looked like something must have happened to it. Do you have any idea what that would be?"

This sent Yao a jolt. He hadn't thought he would be asked about the sheet. It seemed obvious to Yao that Zhao was deliberately going for the crack in his armor. He was really beginning to loathe Zhao.

"I took a short nap there after lunch. Did I wrinkle it up? You can have Xiao Zhang send it here. I promise I'll press it one-hundred percent smooth."

"Oh, no, don't bother. I was just wondering."

"By the way, I was wondering, too—is Xiao Zhang still at your office?"

"She's . . . no! She's not here. It's pretty late now. She must have gone home quite awhile ago."

Hearing Zhao give himself away was hugely pleasing to Yao. "Did you forget she isn't married? Where does she live? Young women are so vulnerable these days. You're her boss. You ought to be taking better care of her."

"You're right . . . you're right."

"She took my call in your office a minute ago."

"That . . . that's not possible!"

"I'm a hundred percent sure it was her. I recognized her voice right away."

"That is so damned strange!"

"What would be strange is if it was anybody besides her answering the phone. Oh, and would you please tell her that it was not very polite for her to answer my call to you the way she did."

He hung up the phone as soon as he finished, leaving Fat Zhao no chance to explain. *Imagine the look on his face right now in front of Xiao Zhang!* Yao thought, actually giggling like a child. The idea that he had put the screws on Zhao exhilarated him.

Damn you, Fat Zhao! Yao swore in his heart. *I bet you're not going to sleep too well tonight!*

YAO SLEPT STRAIGHT through the next day. Evening found him lounging on the couch absorbed in his newspapers and magazines. He had not subscribed to any newspapers until recently. Now he was getting five or six. It seemed to him that the papers were getting more interesting. They're a hodgepodge of stories—*some* of them true, some false. He reasoned that if all the stories were true, reading them would get boring, just the same as knowing they were all completely made up: you'd lose interest. The stories he liked best were half true and half fictional. He believed that what people really wanted, anyway, were equal portions of facts and lies.

At five after eight his wife came in.

He said, "You're home?"

She said, "I'm home."

"Why so late?"

"Had business to take care of for the company."

"Your new boss's business?"

"I suppose you could put it that way."

He could feel the chill, the determined indifference in his wife's voice. She had spoken that way on previous occasions, but he hadn't taken it seriously. This time things were different, though he couldn't say exactly what the difference was. He smiled at her. He did not want to get upset, nor did he want to upset her. He still needed her help.

He asked, "Have you had your dinner?"

She said, "How could I not? It's past eight already."

"Just wondering . . . in case you haven't had anything to eat." He wanted to strike up a conversation. "Where did you have dinner?"

"Yuan Cheng Restaurant."

"That's an expensive place."

"Sure is."

"You escorted your boss?"

"Why do you have to think that I escorted him? Why not the other way around?"

"Well, then, he escorted you?"

"Right."

"So, why?"

"It was nothing. It was like those foreign movies. He said, 'May I have dinner with you,' and I said, 'Of course.'"

"You acted like there was nothing unusual about it?"

"That's right. I did. Is there anything wrong with that?"

"No, there isn't."

Yao laid down the newspaper and turned on the television. He couldn't find anything interesting after going through several channels, so he turned it back off.

His wife had sat down at the opposite end of the couch and

was massaging her face, which she had started to do while he was still talking to her. She appeared to be concentrating.

"You've changed your routine."

She glanced at him but said nothing, continuing to massage.

"Usually you don't do that until you wash up and brush your teeth when you're going to bed."

She shrugged. She stopped massaging and took off her outfit.

He stared at her legs, then said, a bit surprised, "You didn't wear pantyhose when you left home yesterday."

"Our company gives us a pair every week. I put mine on as soon as I got them."

Yao didn't ask any more questions as he mused upon his wife's legs. He knew her answer was a put-off, a delaying tactic, exactly what he had expected from her. He came to the conclusion that people must be dodging and bluffing everywhere all day long. *Fine*, he thought, *learning how to bluff is what people have to do to lead a normal life. Well, I'm learning . . . and not too late.* He now viewed his habits of cautiousness as nothing more than his inability to bluff. But it wasn't such a hard thing to learn after all. He thought about his wife's suspicious behavior and the ways she dodged whenever he questioned her. Whatever facts she was concealing would remain a mystery to him. He gave up any thought of asking her where she had stayed overnight. She would only stall him off again. He recalled how beautiful her legs were, and inevitably compared hers to the rabbit-faced woman's. It seemed to him that Rabbit Face's legs were lovelier, at least to a man like him. His wife's legs were long enough, but the muscles were too tight. Besides, the skin had gotten darker from riding her bicycle to work every day. Rabbit Face's legs were long and delicate. The silky thighs felt so soft and boneless that he could have rolled them into *jiaozi*. Lying together in Zhao Jing-yu's bed with the woman who had clasped that pair of legs around his waist made him feel that he had become part of her body. At that moment, even a gun pointed at his temple couldn't have separated him from her. But what was her name? He had forgotten it completely. He could only remember that her family name was Qu, and she had a face like a rabbit.

Yao's wife took off her pantyhose and left to take a leisurely bath.

He wondered what her boss had thought about her legs. Then a weird, preposterous idea occurred to him: He would like to talk about women's legs with his wife's boss. They could start right away with his wife's legs.

"I'm going to bed, now," his wife said, passing from the bathroom directly into the bedroom.

He got up and followed her into the bedroom. "Can you please make a phone call to Old Zhao for me?" he asked in a voice that all but begged.

"What for? Do you have to have *me* call him?"

He gave her a gender-neutral version of the situation. His wife lay on the bed and listened with no expression on her face. As he talked he began to imagine he was looking down over Qu. His lengthy, restorative sleep that day had energized him. He thought, *If only it could be Qu lying here in this bed!*

She listened quietly until he finished the explanation, then asked, perplexed, "You say that was the person Old Zhao had talked to and wanted to reject? Why did you let yourself get pulled into the middle of it? And now you're trying to get me to mediate for you?"

He came over, sat down on the bed next to her, and stroked her legs. "He had the ball, see, and he kicked it to me."

He could feel the difference in the two women's legs. The other one's were more delicate. It was like comparing percale with silk. If he were ever going to touch the silky legs again, he would have to get his wife to mediate between himself and Zhao.

"You would take anything he kicked to you?"

"I've already taken it."

"Why can't you kick it back to him?"

"Don't you know how crafty Old Zhao is? He scored his point the second he kicked the ball over to me. I can't kick this one back."

"Male or female?"

"What?"

"The *ball.*"

He started to answer "male," but realized right away that couldn't work. She would find out the truth as soon as she called Old Zhao. What a foolish mistake that would have been.

"Female," he said in complete honesty.

His wife stared at him and replied softly, but very significantly, "*Ohhh.*"

"Do not stare at me like that, and don't 'Ohhh' me. This has nothing to do with 'male' or 'female.'"

"What does it have to do with, then?" she asked, still staring at him.

"It has to do with our institute's profitability. This woman would pay the institute a big administrative fee. If it goes for bonuses, I'll get another one hundred twenty to one hundred thirty yuan in my pay each month."

"Oh," she repeated, though from a completely different perspective.

"The only way Old Zhao got to be executive director of the institute was because you recommended him. He's still grateful to you. Just use your public-relations skills. I know he'd never let you down."

"Are you sure?"

"Positive."

"I've never even seen the man, just the photo in his file."

"What difference does that make? You've already gotten acquainted with him on the phone."

Yao was not exaggerating. His wife had become familiar with Zhao Jing-yu, and this was done entirely over the telephone. She chatted with him now and then, even making jokes. She was adept at getting to know men through conversation. This time, though, it would only be for the sake of improving the relationship between Zhao and her husband. Once, she had hoped that someday her husband would be a somebody, a real power within the institute, but she had abandoned that illusion along the way.

"Is she beautiful?"

"Who?"

"That woman."

"Has a face like a rabbit, but a good figure . . . Not as good as yours, of course."

"A face like a rabbit!" She laughed. A large, snow-white flannel bunny had stood poised at the head of their bed for several years. She grabbed it and held it in her hands. She scrutinized it for a moment, then laughed again. "A face like a *rabbit*?"

He had blurted out the rabbit simile before realizing what he was saying. Then he remembered she had been born in the year of the rabbit, and so she liked rabbits. He could think of no other reason why this would be so funny to her—hearing that another woman's face looked like a rabbit's. He felt affronted. After all, the woman who made love with him in Zhao

Jing-yu's office was not a rabbit; she was a woman who happened to have a face like a rabbit, that's all. Women and rabbits are completely different categories. Besides, he was beginning to think it was not so unacceptable if a woman's face resembled a rabbit's.

He withdrew his hand from her leg and looked at her sternly.

She stopped laughing, and asked, "What—are you mad at me?"

He asked back, "What's so funny about what I said?"

Instead of answering directly, she said, "And her legs? . . ."

"I'm not a gymnastics coach," he said. "Why should I pay attention to her legs?"

Ignoring this question, too, she slowly stretched one leg straight upward, inspecting it proudly. "Are her legs more attractive to the male than mine?" she asked.

He leaned toward her and said fiercely, "She doesn't have legs! She's handicapped. Sitting in a wheelchair. Now—are you satisfied?"

He had spoken completely out of anger, without the least intention of lying. And she believed him. She dropped her leg and mumbled, "Well, then . . . that's another story."

"Why? Why is it another story?" He gripped her by the throat, as if he were about to strangle her. As a matter of fact, he did feel like it. He was sure that her boss had praised her legs. Otherwise, she wouldn't be so concerned about another woman's legs, or go on and on about her own.

"Tell me!" He tightened his grip.

"Tell you what?" His wife quivered. Her eyes shone. Her lips glowed red in the subdued light. Her body suddenly glowed with sexual arousal. Obviously she was not frightened at all; rather, she felt excited, even giddy.

"You know damned well what I want to know!" Despite the determination he had mustered, his hands loosened and the fierceness in his voice subsided.

She cupped his face in her hands and began to kiss him frantically. Her kisses were so frenzied that he could hardly breathe, as if she intended to suck the internal organs out of his body and swallow them up. Before his distracted mind knew what was happening, his body had been ignited by the flames of desire that she had kindled. He was unaware of stripping away his clothes or of his wife becoming naked—perhaps she had torn the clothes away from both of them. Above his gaze, on the wall, hung a cheap tapestry depicting the yin and yang. The circle, which was said to represent all things in the universe, began to rotate before his eyes until the two fish inside the circle merged into one blurred image. It suddenly seemed to him that he had achieved a much deeper understanding of the symbol. The accumulating external stimuli plunged him head-long into frenzy. He closed his eyes, imagining that the woman twisting her body on the bed and groaning out of bliss was not his wife but the rabbit-faced woman. He avoided opening his eyes for fear that the fantasy would end. Only by feeding this fantasy could he pretend that what he was doing was making love, and not just having sex.

"Look at me," she begged in between her groans.

He pretended not to hear.

"Open your eyes!"

He kept his eyes closed but began to obey all the other instructions she gave him. She asked him to do this, now that; some of the maneuvers required novel skills. He followed her coaching with intense concentration, like an elementary student in his first phys ed class.

"You're not so stupid at all. . . ." she murmured as praise.

He thought so, too. He smiled with pride and satisfaction, but with his eyes still closed.

"Oh no . . . Something's burning!"

It was the acrid smell of smoke that finally forced his eyes open. He leaned over the edge of the bed—the bottom half of his body still on location—and groped about the floor, thinking he might have thrown a smoldering cigarette butt onto the rug.

"No, not on the floor—it's on the bed lamp. . . ."

He peered up at the lamp. His wife's thin silk underwear lay smoldering hotly over the bulb. It takes some time for a lamp bulb to burn even a piece of very thin fabric. He paused to estimate how long this mattress episode must have lasted and was very surprised to find that it was some kind of record, one he had certainly never attained or even dreamed of before. He wondered whether it was his physical or his mental strength that had sustained him.

Yao then snatched the burning panties away from the lamp and rushed to the bathroom. He threw them into the sink and doused them with cold water.

Falling back down onto the bed, he knew he had returned utterly from nirvana to the real world. Yet he delighted in his gratitude for the rabbit-faced woman. He accepted as proved that fantasy could motivate a person as forcefully as physical strength or intellectual argument. Imagination can satisfy all the deficiencies of the real world, as long as the imagining stays consistent with honest desires. Take a dog as an example: when a dog has no bone to chew on but does have enough imagination, it can satisfy itself just as well by chewing up a piece of wood and digesting that.

"Don't forget to call Old Zhao . . . ," he said. He felt as

spent as if he had just fought an all-out battle. He had consumed so much energy that even his body felt lighter.

He immediately fell asleep.

Part Three

WHEN YAO CHUN-GANG awoke the next morning, it was already past nine o'clock. A short note written by his wife lay on the nightstand. He picked it up and read it: *I've already made that phone call to Old Zhao for you. He agreed to think it over some more. He said he never turned you down completely. You were too impatient and didn't give him time to consider everything.*

Yao Chun-gang reread the note several times over until he felt certain he had not betrayed the rabbit-faced woman. He began to think that this could turn out to be a pretty good day. He lay back in bed and slowly enjoyed a cigarette. *When things are going your way, even the same old brand of cigarettes tastes better,* he thought. He blocked his impulse to call the rabbit-faced woman. It was her fault that he had already lost his temper in front of the one person who should never see such behavior. Anyway, he was in no hurry to hand over the news she was dying to hear. He reasoned that he deserved some kind of recognition of his efforts; but not money, of course. *She's the kind of woman you could never forget, not after that first time together.* Yao felt his craving for her grow by the hour. If he tried to concentrate on some other subject, whatever it was evolved into a new way of thinking about her. Each subsequent thought of her flushed him with another surge of virility.

Stubbing out the cigarette, he got up from bed. After leisurely washing up, brushing his teeth, and having some milk and bread, he turned on the television. They were giving news from the stock markets in Shanghai and Shenzhen—how active the trading had been, quotations on some featured stocks. Then a TV anchorman interviewed a few lucky upstarts who had just struck it rich playing the markets. Yao felt himself burning with jealousy and resentment. How he wished he could have got in on it, too, but Shenzhen and Shanghai were too far away. In Beijing they had sold stocks only two times and only at a few specific places. He had heard that those places were jammed with people. He just didn't have the energy to go and stand in such a long line in such hot weather. Neither did he have enough cash to buy any stock offerings. His joint savings-account balance only ran to four digits, starting with a three. He felt jealous—jealous and resentful.

He used to curse under his breath when people talked about stocks at the institute. While they were making money, he was stuck with organizing political study sessions on topics like "Stick with Socialism!" He would love to show them a real program on socialist education! Attendance would be mandatory for everyone in China who had a bank account with more than 50,000 yuan! . . . No, make it more than 30,000 yuan . . . No, 20,000 yuan. He would make each session drone on for eight or ten years. The first lesson would include confiscating all the students' personal property. He had read in *Reference News* that the total sum on deposit in private accounts in Chinese banks had surpassed 100 billion yuan. Further, most of this money was held by one- to two-tenths of one percent of the population. A 100 billion yuan! *Let's see: if you divide that up among 1.2 billion Chinese, how much would each one get? . . .*

Yao switched to a different channel. He didn't know what the program was, except that it was about stocks and had interviews. Some fatso with a beaming face was crowing to the audience about how he started out with a couple thousand yuan and ended up with a couple of million. Yao angrily turned off the television and grabbed the previous day's paper. Even it was full of news that made him jealous. It seemed that the media were doing everything they could to get on his nerves and depress him. He dearly wished that someone would come to him and tell him how to subdue the panic that was growing stronger and fiercer in his heart—show him exactly what to do to find a brighter future.

Just as he was thinking along these lines, someone actually did knock at the door. Yao jumped up from the couch nearly overjoyed and went to see who it was.

The caller was a male stranger about Yao's own age.

"Who are you looking for?"

"You."

"And, you are—?"

"From the Bureau of Public Security."

This gave Yao a jolt. He was certain he hadn't broken any laws. But when he recalled the rabbit-faced woman, as he was doing all the time now, he became unsettled. Had she gotten him mixed up with criminals? Maybe she'd been accused by the wife of one of the men she had been comforting. She could have confessed and turned over the names of every man she had sex with, including Yao. That may not land him in jail, but when the news got around, it would definitely ruin his reputation. Oh, God! Don't let her be involved in some murder-for-love case and make him submit written testimony—or worse, appear in court. Well, if this was the outcome, then nothing would have been worth fooling around with that woman. He couldn't imagine his wife not demanding a divorce. It would be out of the question for him to stay on as the vice director. *That damned, phony, sleazy bitch!* He cursed her in his heart, taking all that he had imagined as actual truth. A chill gripped his body.

"May I . . . see your ID?"

"Certainly." The stranger took a card out of his inside suit-coat pocket.

Yao had barely accepted the card when the stranger said, "Shouldn't I come on inside?"

"Yes, of course. Please . . ." Yao asked him in. "Please sit down."

After the visitor had settled into a comfortable chair, Yao sat down and began looking over the ID card.

"I think . . . you gave me the wrong ID. This isn't—"

The visitor had given him a company's employee ID.

"Did I?" The visitor took the card from Yao and glanced at it. "Oh yeah." He casually handed Yao another card. "This is the one I meant."

"This . . . isn't it . . . either."

"Oh, sorry. Sorry." The visitor retrieved the second ID and took out a third one.

It wasn't a proper ID, either.

Yao concluded that his visitor must be an undercover agent; an ordinary person could never carry so many employee ID cards. Only an undercover agent would need to conceal his true identity. Yao's sense of the seriousness of the situation grew sharper. Did that rabbit-faced woman get him mixed up in some kind of trouble over foreign dealings? He was all but convinced that he had really hit some bad luck, and he became even more anxious.

"Look—that's okay," said Yao. "Don't worry about it. Just go ahead with your questions. I . . . I'll answer everything honestly." He returned the third ID card reverently. He noted that each card had been more impressive than the previous one.

The stranger burst into laughter. When he finished laughing, he patted Yao on the knees, then said in sober earnestness, "Don't be nervous."

Yao smiled awkwardly and said, "I'm . . . no. I'm not nervous."

The visitor offered Yao a cigarette. "Let's have a smoke first."

Yao snatched out his own cigarettes and offered them to the visitor. "Have one of mine, please."

Without any hesitation, the visitor took one of Yao's cigarettes and put it to his lips. Yao lit the visitor's cigarette, then his own. After a moment the visitor looked at Yao attentively and asked, "Have you ever taken any bribes?"

"No, never. Why would anyone come to an institute like mine with a bribe? I stay honest without even trying."

"Have you ever bribed anyone else, then?"

"Well, this . . . No. It's only me and my wife here—no kids, so we're not tempted in that area. We've never gotten involved in anything that would take a bribe to get done."

"What about illegal merchandising or foreign trade?"

"No, no. Definitely no. We only have ordinary social connections. I would sort of like to get into some kind of buying and selling, but what business connections could I or my wife work through?" Yao's words sounded despairing, as if he were a pathetic pauper.

"Well, okay then. Let's go on to your 'private' affairs."

"This . . . well, this . . . ah."

"What? Is this going to be embarrassing for you?"

"Well, what man could be one hundred percent the gentleman? I'm no exception. That kind of indiscretion—I can't say it's never actually happened." Yao froze with the cigarette poised in his hand. He shuddered to think that this might be the bull's-eye the visitor was aiming for.

The stranger laughed loudly again, slapping him on the knees one more time.

"Yao Chun-gang, don't you recognize me at all? I knew it was you as soon as you opened the door."

The visitor leaned toward Yao, looking him directly in the eyes to make it easier for Yao to recognize him.

"But then . . . you're not a—"

He still had no idea who the visitor was, and he was thoroughly rattled by the interrogation.

"I'm Sun Ke, your middle-school classmate. Don't you remember me? I was kidding you. When I saw that you'd completely forgotten about me, I pretended to be from the Bureau of Public Security."

"Sun Ke?"

"I was the assistant leader of the school's Mao Zedong Thought propaganda team. My nickname was Pigeon. Remember?"

"Oh! Why, you! . . . You've changed so damned much, you completely fooled me. I really thought you were a plainclothes investigator!" He laughed loudly to mask his exasperation. It would be unforgivable to explode in anger at a former classmate who has dropped by out of the blue for a visit. "We haven't seen each other for over twenty years, have we?"

"Right. Over twenty. I heard you're the director now."

"*Assistant* director. I just pass myself off as the director. How did you find out where I live?"

"I had a get-together for our old classmates at my place yesterday. I contacted everyone I could locate, and over two-thirds of them showed up. Your name came up, of course; you used to be our class monitor."

"I really haven't done so well. I'm too ashamed to get back together with old classmates."

"Come on, how can you say you're not doing too well? That institute you're in — isn't it a department-level office?"

"No, it's a bureau . . . a chief bureau."

The last part was a lie. Yao immediately reproached himself. What was the point of pumping up his institute?

"Well, then you're a bureau-level director. Not too many of our middle-school classmates have gotten that far. One of the guys was telling me about your institute yesterday."

"Who was that?"

Yao almost never had any contact with his classmates from middle school. However, he knew that some of them had really made something of themselves — scholars, professors, entrepreneurs, businessmen — and had become conspicuous, upper-tier consumers. He had always tortured himself with feelings of inferiority. It only made matters worse to turn forty-five and be passed over for editor in chief in favor of Young Zhang. And yet Yao had come to understand that he did have ambitions, and other desires. Indeed, he was not the kind of man who was so easily satisfied. Therefore, he was curious to know the identity of the old classmate who had known he was at the China Psychological History Research Institute. He hoped it was a female classmate.

"Who?" Sun Ke tapped his scalp. "I can't remember. It was a guy, I know that. Not too many of the girls would have talked about you. You were too proud back in those days! They all kept a polite distance. Anyway, I dropped by to see you at your institute this morning. Your executive director received me. Nice person. Very polite to me. He drew a map to your home for me; otherwise, I could never have found it."

"How are you doing?"

"Well—that's a long story. You probably noticed from my ID cards that I'm running quite a few companies. Business is expanding. Every one of my companies has assets in the tens of millions and lands a big deal almost every month. Once you have a reputation for that kind of success, they'll come knocking at your door for business, whether you're interested or not. You know, I'm starting to get tired of it all. Every year I spend at least three months out of the country. Have to do it. That's where the business is."

Yao began to feel jealous of his old classmate, though not too jealous. He envied people like Sun Ke who could buy private cars. People like that traveled abroad as easily as regular people visited other provinces. They stayed in five-star hotels. That kind of luxury would be impossible if Sun Ke were running a state-owned company; he would be getting five hundred to six hundred yuan a month, maybe more than a taxi driver, and he could never afford a private car. Of course, the managers at state-owned companies got to travel first class, in soft berths on trains; they might even have a chauffeured limousine, but such perquisites came nowhere near to compensating for the hours they put in. Yao thought it just wasn't worth the trouble. He would never spend his life that way.

"Where does your wife work?" Yao asked.

"To tell you the truth—I'm on my third marriage," laughed Sun Ke. "This one is a pop singer. I met her one evening when I was taking some business associates out to a hotel lounge, and she was singing. I kept thinking what a pretty girl she was, really delightful, and what a sweet voice she had. I had a big basket of flowers delivered to her. We got to know each other after that. Anyway, she doesn't sing in public anymore. Only for me at home. She's twenty-one years younger than me. Still a little girl. One thing, though: *this* young lady definitely was *not* going to just sit around at home. I thought, well, she's not a bird that I feed and keep in a cage, so I let her take over one of my businesses, a clothing company, just to give her something to do. I didn't care if she made money or lost it. At the worst it would only come to three hundred thousand or four hundred thousand yuan. So I thought, okay, she can have fun playing boss. What I did not expect was that she'd turn over a two hundred thousand yuan profit her first year. I started to think she was turning into a workaholic. Before long I'd be married to a business executive instead of a wife. Seems like all girls nowadays have a head for business, unless they're retarded or something. Give one of them fifty or sixty thousand and you'd be dead wrong to think they couldn't turn it into a hundred and fifty or sixty thousand in a year. They are *born* shrewd and tough. They separate men from their money—and the men love it! No wonder people say, 'In China—strong female, weak male.' That's one of China's specialties.

"Anyway, my two ex-wives are both gorgeous. And why not? I'm a big shot. When I married them, they were the most submissive little darlings. But before long, they turned into something else. Like my third wife, they wouldn't stay at home, either. They soft-talked me until they got their way. How could I say no? Once they got set up in one of my operations, it was like they had found themselves. The next thing I knew, there's my wife taking care of business like a pro. But that wasn't what I wanted. What I wanted was a sweet, tender little lady that I could take care of, and hug, and love. Both times, when I told them I was thinking about a divorce, their attitude was that if I wanted out of the marriage, I'd have to give them complete ownership of the companies they were running. I'm pretty sure they didn't plan to go into business before they married me, but they got confident later. When things came to a head, I ended up telling both of them, 'Well, business and money go together. Name the amount and I'll give it to you. After all, you've been a good wife.' And what do you think *they* said? My first wife said, 'Money is money; business is business. That business I built up for you is the proof of how much money I'm worth to you.' My second wife said the very same thing, like they had been in cahoots!

"What else can I say? I gave my first wife a store that sells car accessories. That included a one-hundred-square-meter commercial lot and seven or eight employees. I gave my second wife an advertising company, the same amount of office space, and told her she could have any of the employees that wanted to go to work for her. They all went with her. Both of these women were millionaires in five or six years. They both live in big houses. Both have big cars, top of the line. And both of them got married again, too, to intellectuals—real celebrities, not some graduate student. I guess now that they're millionaires, they deserve the best. My first wife's husband is a middle-aged economist, a Ph.D. My second wife's husband is a writer; he's making a name for himself and is four years younger than she is. She liked the way he obeyed her like a child; she could put up with the little bit of fame he had, and married him. I've seen both men; they're better looking than I am. Both my exes have kids now. All three of our families have stayed on good terms. We go places together over weekends and holidays. I have three kids—two girls and a boy, the best combination. My first two wives each had a daughter, and my third wife had a son. When we all get together, nobody can tell which child is whose, or which men and women are the married couples.

"Sometimes my two exes come to me about business problems they're dealing with. I always do what I can to help. The two of them get along great with my third wife, just like sisters. Once in a while, one of them will catch me alone and we'll have a quick romp in the sack, just for old time's sake. My wife just winks at it. Never gets jealous. Once I even asked her what she thought about it. She said, 'Hooray for them! It proves you're a good man; otherwise, they wouldn't be hanging around after the divorce. They stay because of the feelings you and they have kept for each other. I respect those feelings. You're a big shot. You have hookers throwing themselves at you.' See how open-minded she is? It's like it has nothing to do with her. But she's completely scrupulous about herself. She'd never think of cheating on me. A wife like that must be the best thing a man can have.

"That's why money is such a wonderful thing. If you have money, good luck will come knocking on your door. If you have money, even divorce is just a detour to other pleasures. I'm pretty sure my ex-wives' husbands know that we still have something going on. Money keeps them silent, willingly silent. What's so great about being a writer? Can he make a living off his royalties? It's his wife's advertising company that's paying the bills. With that kind of support, couldn't anyone take the time to turn out elegant literature? What's so fantastic about an economics Ph.D.? Not too many of them are going to marry a wife that can make several hundred thousand yuan a year. Okay—say they don't like being cheated on. They can go ahead and get a divorce. When a woman has money, it won't take her any time at all to find a husband more tolerant of her tastes.

"You know, something I expected after both divorces was that each wife would burn out trying to run a business without me, but I was wrong. They look younger than ever, like they're radiating health. There isn't any knack for making money. It can be very difficult when you start out. Say you've only got a hundred yuan and you want to turn it into a thousand—that can seem like an impossible dream. If you have a thousand and want to turn it into ten thousand, you can do it, but it won't come easy. You'll be playing a few tricks on people. But—if you have a hundred thousand, or several hundred thousand, and you concentrate on simply making money, and you grab the chance when you see it, and you utilize every resource open to you, well, then it's not too hard to make really, really big profits . . . that is, for anybody who isn't retarded. When you have a million, especially when a woman has a million, especially a woman who knows how to please a man and really turn him on—when a person like that has a million to work with, making money is one big, happy game. You can wake up in the morning and find out you've picked up another couple hundred thousand. My relationship with my ex-wives is more than simply the man-woman kind. We have economic relationships. That's the basis for all relationships. Conforms to Marx's theory, doesn't it? The economics of our relationships is mutual benefit. Sometimes when they can't land the deal they want, I offer to help. When we split the profit, I take the bigger share; sometimes I let them have more. I'm loyal to my friends, and they are sensible partners. The Chinese people, our generation—what do we need with all that emotional relationship stuff? Without the money to hold things together, no emotional relationship is unbreakable. . . ."

As Sun Ke talked on, Yao nodded his head, like a graduate student receiving enlightenment from an illustrious professor.

When Sun Ke finally stopped, Yao asked, "Are you thirsty? Let me get you some tea."

Sun Ke shook his head. "No, no. I won't be here long. The car is waiting outside."

Yao asked, "Sun Ke, your businesses—everything, all of it belongs to you?"

"Who else would it belong to? I've worked and sweated for seventeen years. Anything I make is mine to keep. But you know, Chun-gang, I'm getting tired of making money. With tens of millions of yuan, you can't exactly run through all of it overnight. I ought to just try to enjoy myself as much as I can. Leave a few million to my children, in case they can't take care of themselves. I'm not managing the whole shebang anymore. I have other people running the day-to-day. I don't even care that much if they're managing things all that well or not. Even if I handed everything over to an idiot, it would still take a few years to lose tens of millions."

It finally dawned on Yao that Sun Ke was talking about those new, home-based businesses—only his were really, really big home-based businesses; and he had tens of millions of yuan . . . and it was all his to keep! The fact that a private individual could accrue such a vast personal fortune shocked Yao into regarding his former classmate in a new light. To have that kind of money would be worth dying for. Yao had heard about characters like Sun Ke, read about them in the newspapers and magazines; but today one of them dropped in on him and was sitting right there in front of him in real life. This time the arrow of another's accomplishments struck the bull's-eye of Yao's jealousy. This time, though, it was no longer jealousy of the usual kind; it was jealousy escalated to ferocity by a newfound clarity of purpose. People say that jealousy will drive a man to kill; at this point, murder was boiling in Yao's heart. He was ready to kill this former classmate—*tear him apart and stomp on the pieces!*

"Look . . . I mean, well, Sun Ke: can you give me a job? I wouldn't need much. Two or three thousand a month would be fine with me. . . ."

Yao's murderous urges notwithstanding, Sun Ke remained serenely intact. It was Yao's dignity that lay torn and trampled.

"You?" His old classmate squinted at him briefly, then spoke calmly. "Two or three thousand a month is not such a high salary, but I would never hire you. And it's not because you're overqualified, either. You're not good enough to work for me. My employees are all business geniuses, the most promising young people. I start fresh college graduates at fifteen hundred a month . . . because I know they'll make hundreds of thousands for me later. But what could you do if you were working for me? People like you were spoiled by the old system. Give you a cup of tea, a pack of cigarettes, and you'll while away a whole day at your office. Reading newspapers and holding meetings—that's your idea of work. Laziness is second nature for your kind. Your job at your institute coddles you. You're like pigs lounging in clover. You have high minds but no talent. You're all good-for-nothings.

"Today the consumer economy is coming alive. When the economy wakes up, people like you are going to be the first ones shown to the door. Even farmers grow grain and vegetables on every square meter of land they can find. In the off-season, they sell things in their town market or take odd jobs. But what can you do? Even if you were to walk away from your cushy institute, would you be physically capable of doing anything anyone would want to pay for? People who carry on research in high-tech areas can make a discovery or invent something useful. They get a reward; they file a patent. But you guys don't know a thing about high technology. You call yourselves intellectuals, but you're science illiterates! Go take a look at what you have to offer anybody. How could I hire someone like you?"

"Right. *Right!* You're right: I was spoiled by the old system. I have picked up a lot of bad habits. I guess I am a good-for-nothing, as you said. But . . . for an old classmate's sake, couldn't you please consider hiring me? Just think about it. . . ."

In this manner Yao shamelessly tried to sell himself. He knew what he was doing was shameful, but in light of Zhao Jing-yu's nebulous plans, the prospect of working for Sun Ke seemed all the more compelling. Yao used to scorn people who left their jobs in state-owned businesses for private enterprise. He thought they were shortsighted, impetuous; young people are always that way. But now he found such beliefs shattered by his old buddy Sun Ke's words. As his visitor rambled on again, Yao savored the possibilities that would spring from an entirely new lifestyle, a life that would never bring him the embarrassment of an empty wallet.

"No." Sun Ke shook his head determinedly. "Forget it. No way. I'd never hire you. If you need some money, come and see me. I can give you a thousand one time. That's nothing, about as much as I spend taking two people out to dinner. But I can't hire you. I just can't hire people who are useless to me. That's my policy."

Damn you and *your policy!* thought Yao.

Sun Ke glanced at his watch. It was a big, thick watch, with a glittering gold band. Yao had seen that brand displayed in a case at an upscale department store. He remembered the price: 130,000 yuan.

Yao said, "Forget about time. You'll have to stay here for lunch. We haven't seen each other for over twenty years. I can't let you go without having lunch. We still have a lot to talk about."

"No, no; I've got to get going. I just meant to drop in for a quick visit. I've already stayed too long." Sun Ke stood up. "I've got business to take care of." Sun Ke paused for a moment. "Oh, by the way, my holding company has a subsidiary here in Beijing. The general manager is my wife's brother. If you ever need a car for an emergency, just call him." Sun Ke took out a wallet of business cards, pulled one out of its plastic sleeve, and tossed it on the table. "Here's his card."

"Do you really have to hurry?" Yao was feeling bereft, even abandoned, by Sun Ke's departure.

"Yes, I really do."

"Can I . . . can I have one of *your* cards?"

"Well—*ha ha*—I don't really think it's necessary. You wouldn't have any use for my card. I'm hard to find. You know—here in China today, somewhere else tomorrow." Sun was letting himself out of the apartment as he spoke.

As he walked, Yao tagged along behind, following him all the way downstairs and out of the apartment building, mumbling conventional niceties as if he were an old lady seeing off a social caller. Sun Ke abruptly ended the conversation. Without shaking Yao's hand good-bye, he opened the door and got into the waiting car. The chauffeur immediately drove away.

"You son of a *bitch*!" Yao cursed under his breath. How he wished there could be a bomb in the car, a bomb Yao could set off and blow Sun Ke and his car sky-high, blow Sun's body to bits. . . .

YAO WONDERED WHO could have told Sun Ke where he worked. And what kind of enjoyment—which could only have been minuscule—had led Sun Ke to take time out from his busy life to track Yao down, first at his institute and then at his home? Could he really have been prompted by nostalgia, as he claimed? Yao doubted that. It is true that people in their forties tend to develop deeper emotional needs, especially as their current situations provide less and less comfort. They search for any small thing that can remind them of the old days. Just like an old woman when she rediscovers a bundle of forgotten patches in the corner of a closet, people in their forties cherish any old junk from the past that they can find. That is why there are so many social organizations that help old classmates, such as the "educated youth," get back in touch with each other. The organizers usually are the new millionaires, naturally, since nothing is going to get done without money. Maybe Sun Ke was trying to become the chairman of some social organization. *So what if he does?* thought Yao. *Hmmm, what if he needs to get my approval for something? Wait a minute . . .* Yao thought he had it. *Sun Ke still remembers that I was our class monitor back then.* Well, if Sun Ke were trying to finagle his way around the class monitor so he could get to be chairman of the social organization, then he must have a pretty sore conscience! Obviously he wanted to make up for it by paying Yao a visit. After another moment's reflection, Yao dropped the idea. Sun Ke had not even said a word about being in any social organization.

The more he tried to piece things together, the more confused he became. He would have continued pondering over this for who knows how long if the telephone had not rung.

"Is this Comrade Yao Chun-gang's home?"

Yao heard a woman's voice speaking faintly from the telephone receiver, as if the call had come from hundreds or thousands of miles away. However, he could make out what she was saying.

"Yes, this is Yao Chun-gang. Is that Qu . . . um, Qu . . ."

"I am Qu Su-juan." The tone of voice was intimate.

"I knew it was you. I recognized your voice right away."

"*Oh* . . . well, thank you very much for not forgetting me."

"How could I ever? Where are you calling from?"

"My home. I really wanted to call you yesterday, but every time I started to, I hung up the receiver."

"Now, why would that be?" His voice turned suggestive when she said she was calling from home.

"I don't know. I couldn't tell you why."

"Well, I've been waiting for you to call. You know, your voice has a quality all its own. I recognized you right away."

"*Reeeally?*" The playfulness in the way she drew out the word was unmistakable.

"Sure did!"

The caller laughed and then lowered her voice. "Why didn't you call me first, then?"

"Because yesterday there weren't any results to report about your case. Of course, I don't want you to pick up your phone and get all excited and then hang up disappointed. But now I can tell you to get ready for something good because it's going to happen! There's an eighty- to ninety-percent chance that I'll get an agreement soon. I . . . even got into a shouting match with Director Zhao over this."

He exaggerated the significance of his last sentence.

"Hello, Yao? Yao Chun-gang? Excuse me for interrupting. Do you have me confused with someone else? I was your middle-school classmate Qu Su-juan. I sat next to you in class the first two years. Then I went out to the countryside, just like you. I haven't seen you since then."

Oh no. It wasn't the rabbit-faced woman, the one that made his heart beat and his body sizzle. *Qu Su-juan* . . . Oh yes. They had been classmates; used to sit next to each other the first two years in middle school. She went to the countryside first, and they never saw each other again after that. *What in the hell is going on today!* thought Yao, by now totally bewildered. *Did she really have to call me right now? . . . And have the same family name!*

"Oh—Qu Su-juan, yes . . . I have a colleague that has the same family name, and her first name is similar to yours, too. I've been expecting her to call me today. About business, of course. Your voice is a lot like hers. Big mistake! Ha ha! Well . . . I'll bet there's a good reason for you calling me after twenty years, isn't there?"

"Nothing special, really." Her playful voice had changed to a disinterested monotone. "Did Sun Ke come and visit you?"

"I just now walked him out to his car."

"Did you two have a nice talk?"

"Well, how should I put it? I wasted a whole hour. All he did was talk talk talk. Now that I think about it, I have no idea why he did come to see me. It still doesn't make any sense."

"I was afraid something like that might happen. I'm sorry. I'm the one who told him the name of your institute."

"Oh. That's all right. But, so, how did you know that I'm at the psychological institute?"

"I'd rather not say. However, not only do I know you're at the institute, I know you recently became the vice director. Yesterday some of our old classmates had a reunion. Sun Ke organized it. He asked everyone where you worked and how you were doing. Nobody there knew. I thought he seemed genuine, so I told him everything I knew. He wrote it down in his memo book. After that, when he was pretty drunk, he started talking nonsense. He was cursing you. He said he missed all the old classmates—except you. Not only that, he said he *hated* you. He said he was going to get you good. Then I was sorry I told him you were at the institute, but it was too late. Before people started to leave, he said he was going to go see you at your institute. We were all telling him to calm down and not do anything he'd be sorry for later, but he insisted that he was going to find you tomorrow—today, I guess—and tell you where to get off. I wanted to call you yesterday to let you know what was coming, but it was already past eight. So I called your institute the first thing this morning. Someone told me you were out on sick leave. They gave me a phone number for your office, but it was the wrong number. I tried to call again, but nobody would answer the phone. I called the institute again about ten minutes ago. This time your director took the call himself, and I was able to get the right number. Oh, I just knew it would be too late to warn you. I kind of feel sorry for causing you all this trouble. Thank God he didn't really go to your institute and cuss you out like he said he was going to do."

"So, he got drunk yesterday," said Yao, "don't take it too seriously. Maybe we didn't see eye to eye, but we showed enough respect for each other. Remember, I am a bureau-level director and a scholar in psychology. Upstarts like Sun Ke, once they're rich, start to get overbearing, forget where they came from. Of course, in their own mind they know they really are inferior. Put people like him in front of someone who is a high-ranking Party cadre *and* a scholar, well—you'll see them tucking in their horns!"

"Yes, I totally believe that," said Qu Su-juan, her voice filled with genuine admiration. Qu Su-juan had admired him since their middle-school days. He could picture her better now: a short, skinny girl, stunted growth from poor nutrition; incurably shy; one leg slightly crippled from infantile paralysis. She studied all the time but never got good grades. Several days before final exams, she would get all worked up for fear that she would fail and be held back a grade. But each time she eked out a promotion to the next grade. Yao had been among the best students in the class. It was only natural for her to admire him in those days. What he hadn't expected was that she would keep her admiration alive for more than twenty years. She must have secretly imagined him as her prince. He felt somewhat touched by that.

"So, how have you been, Qu Su-juan?"

"Pretty good."

"Well, where are you working these days?"

"In a grocery store."

"Why don't you come and visit me when you have some time."

"Sure, if I'm welcome."

"How could you not be?"

Yao was regaining the self-esteem that Sun Ke had dashed. While he was painting himself as a bureau-level director and a scholar for Qu Su-juan, his manner became more reserved, more discretionary in the words he used. He finally had a new, good reason to feel superior.

Yao asked whether Sun Ke had been boasting about himself. She said that he hadn't. Admiration still softened her words.

"This is so damned unfair!" Yao's cynicism returned.

Both parties were silent for a moment.

"In middle school, that Sun Ke was a total nobody!" fumed Yao. "He even stole the class treasury once, didn't he? His personal hygiene was just as bad, too. Every time the school principal came around to check up on classroom sanitation, our teacher had me go out and stop Sun Ke at the gate so he wouldn't pull down our rating. He cheated on tests; we caught him once and ran him out of the classroom. His moral behavior wasn't too commendable, either; always trying to impress girls."

Yao was glad to be getting to even the score with the man he had just seen off, the man who had provoked such jealousy. He wished he were at a TV station doing a live broadcast, so that 1.2 billion Chinese could watch the sniveling nobody be exposed for what he was: a vulgar nouveau riche!

The woman at the other end of the line remained hesitantly silent.

"Hello, are you still there?" Yao asked. "Why don't you say something?"

"I don't know what to say. I can't remember any of those things. Why have you remembered everything so clearly?"

"Because real life is so unfair. Seeing Sun Ke again brought back all those memories from the past."

"You can't just decide that real life is unfair, Chun-gang. Although Sun Ke stayed around in the city and got out of going to the countryside, he still had a rough time. He went five or six years without a regular job, and . . . that poor family of his . . . you can see how hard their life must have been. In the last ten years, after we all came back to the city and started going after college diplomas, good jobs, and titles—a house for ourselves— he's been traveling around dealing on his own. Whether he was making money or losing money, he still had to pretend he was happy with all kinds of people. He's had to live with a lot less security than we have. Did you notice that one finger on his left hand is missing? It was cut off by an underworld gang when he was working on a deal in Guangxi. While we've been enjoying our peaceful lives here, he took his sweat money down south to try his luck. He traded in real estate and stocks. He finally got rich down there. He settled down to live in the south. So now he's come back to his hometown to see his old classmates and people he knew—friends and enemies—to let everybody know that he is a somebody now. Anyone in his place would've done the same thing. . . ."

Yao couldn't recall later exactly when he hung up the phone; it was definitely before she was finished talking. He sank wearily onto the sofa. He sat there for quite a while completely at a loss.

The man Yao had just seen off had good reason to loathe him. As a monitor in middle school, Yao was in a position over Sun Ke. In fact, he humiliated the boy in front of everyone repeatedly. It was even possible that Sun Ke was innocent of stealing the class treasury. There was no evidence at all to prove that he was the culprit. Nevertheless, Yao Chun-gang talked some of the students into testifying that Sun Ke was guilty. This setup fell short of getting Sun Ke expelled from school, but everyone looked down on him after that. During the Cultural Revolution, Yao became the head of the school's Red Guards. He repeatedly blocked Sun Ke from joining the organization, and Sun Ke never once got a chance to wear the red armband.

At this point Yao's musings returned to the present: a flat, no more than thirty square meters at best, and some outdated furniture—a sagging sofa, a twice-repaired TV set, and the refrigerator, all of which he had acquired at wholesale prices through a "back door." It's true that he had a college diploma, albeit from a correspondence school—rather like the vice director's title that carried no real power, not to mention the uncertainty about how long he would even have that; he had a monthly salary of 140 lousy yuan; he had reached the advanced age of forty-five; and he had a wife who had stopped being faithful to him, stayed out overnight, and who could present him with divorce papers at any time. Somehow this was how his life had turned out lock, stock, and barrel. He felt overwhelmed with a sense of loss, dejection, misery. As he acknowledged these emotions one after the other, they merged and mushroomed into a monstrous panic—a panic driven by stark reality and what it offered him in terms of future prospects, his life, his very self. Though not new to him, this sense of panic had never before been so palpable. Sun Ke's visit had provoked it, made it ferocious, as if it had bitten Yao in the neck. When he mustered the nerve to beg Sun Ke for a job, he had no idea that his former classmate was taking revenge on him. Because of his superior position, Sun Ke was able to bait Yao's jealousy and then take his revenge through subtle niceties. Had Yao known about Sun Ke's true purpose, he would never have humiliated himself by begging. If only he had not gotten jealous; then Sun Ke would never have had his satisfaction. But Yao was jealous of Sun Ke. He was jealous to death. He was choked with jealousy inside and out. Even thinking about it in retrospect stifled his breathing.

"What could you do? . . . You're a good-for-nothing. . . . If you need money, come and see me; I can give you a thousand one time. . . . But I can't hire you. I just can't hire people who are useless to me. . . ."

Those words from Sun Ke had wounded him like nails pounded into his heart. A momentary wave of numbness that had overtaken Yao was quickly followed by a jolt of physical pain so sharp that it ought to have left him bleeding. Even that goofy Qu Su-juan, his middle-school-days admirer, was defending Sun Ke!

Yao got up and grabbed a bottle. It was Maotai, China's finest rice liqueur, left over from a business banquet he had attended with Zhao Jing-yu. As the banquet party was breaking up, Fat Zhao pressed the bottle into Yao's hand and told him, "Take this home. It's real Maotai. Two hundred yuan a bottle." Yao did not appreciate getting table leftovers as a perquisite, especially in front of the other guests; they must have wondered if he was financially troubled. But Zhao pushed the milk-white bottle to him, refusing to take no for an answer. Would Fat Zhao become another Sun Ke in six more years? Yao understood better than anyone that Zhao had no interest at all in psychology; in fact, the old man was disdainful of it. Even Fat Zhao himself would not deny this. He was obviously sailing the psychological institute as if it were his personal yacht, piloting it toward the gilded port of his choosing. The question for Yao was, when would Old Zhao throw him overboard?

Yao's morbid apprehensions consumed the afternoon. Neither drinking nor smoking brought him any peace. When his wife came in, he was stretched out completely drunk on the sofa, his legs and feet, still in their shoes, sprawled across the tea table. She glanced at the empty bottle and smiled ruefully.

"I suppose this is how you're going to open the drama."

"Hunh? Wha' drama?" His words were barely intelligible.

"The divorce play. Act One: you show me you don't want to go on living the way we were. Act Two: cold war. Last act: legal separation. Well, we don't have to stay for the whole show! Thank God we don't have children."

"It's all because of you!" He suddenly had a real enemy he could zero in on.

"No! Because of you!" His wife was not about to be outdone. She was even more determined than he to win this battle.

"Well, my do'tor said was *your* pro'lem!"

"My doctor said it was yours! Don't tell me you really thought your 'thirty-second miniseries' were going to take me anywhere!"

She had attacked his most vulnerable area, from which he saw no option but to retreat. "Okay. My pro'lem. My prob . . . blem."

His wife let him escape. She stripped to the skin as she had done on the previous day and went to take a bath. Her dress and pantyhose lay on the floor where they landed. The bra landed on his face.

He remained stoically silent, though he felt mortified.

"Didn't you know the light burned out in here?" she asked.

"No. I haven't used the bathroom."

She left the door partly open so she could find her way in the darkness. He heard her using the toilet, then flushing. Suddenly she shrieked and ran out of the bathroom. In an instant she stood before him, completely naked, arms akimbo.

"The toilet's stopped up!" she yelled. "And you didn't even do anything about it?"

"I tol' you I never used it. How would I know?"

"Oh! You—"

"You come home and nothing suits you. Then you try t' pick a fight." He was speaking piteously, as though he were the one who took the blame for everything at home.

She gave out a snort of exasperation but stood motionless, her feet dripping wet, obviously from the toilet overflow.

"Honey, coul' you please try to be just a li'l more patient? I got a bad headache. Jus' go in and unstop it, and clean it up. Just say you're taking care of me till I'm feeling better. Who hasn't had their toilet stop up? It's no big deal."

He was playing openly for her sympathies. The disastrous experiences of the day had so racked him that the thought of spending the night on the couch was unbearable but nevertheless exactly what he was going to get if he didn't get her to brighten up. What's more, he was getting hungry and wanted her to cook him something for dinner. He looked up at her with the tenderest face he could muster.

She opened her mouth to speak, but words would not come. Silently she walked back to the bathroom.

"How could you throw a pair of panties in the toilet?" she shouted.

"Did I?"

He was almost certain that he had thrown the burning panties into the sink. After more study, he recalled that indeed they had landed in the sink. It was only later, when he was finished in the bathroom and was leaving, that he dropped the panties into the toilet but forgot to flush them down. If he had, it would have backed up on him instead.

"Don't act like you didn't have anything to do with it!"

"How else was I supposed to put them out?"

"Are you telling me the toilet was the only place you could throw them?"

"Okay, *okay!* My mistake. Stop yelling at me. I promise I won't do it again."

"Again? What next time? Do you think I'm ever going to flatter you again like I did yesterday? You're dreaming!"

Now he really had a headache. He struggled to his feet and began to tidy up the room. It had gone ignored for quite a few days—dust lay on everything—but he was determined to act like a good husband if that was what it would take to please his wife.

After her bath she picked up the clothes she had cast off earlier and put them back on. When she saw him cleaning up the room, a look of forgiveness fell over her face.

"What should we have for dinner?" she asked.

"Whatever you want to cook."

"I could make fried bean-sauce noodles? We're out of vegetables."

"Sure."

After a moment she asked, "That rabbit-faced woman's business—did you take care of it? When I talked to Old Zhao on the phone yesterday, I got the feeling that he'd like to do you this favor."

"You seem to be interested in it yourself. Why is that?"

"Why else would I care? You said you could pick up an extra hundred yuan every month."

"I'll go over all the details with Old Zhao tomorrow . . . at the office."

"You need to take him up on this. It'll be good for you, too." She opened her purse, emptied it out on the table, and began to sort through her receipts and loose money. "Was someone here today?"

"No."

"Then whose card is this on the table?" It lay face down, showing the English version printed on the back. She picked up the card and tried to sound out the words, but her scant knowledge of English failed her.

"Oh, well, one person did stop by. A *nobody*, not a somebody. He was a middle-school classmate of mine, the last person in the world anyone would ever notice. He had made some money in the south. He said he owns a subsidiary outfit in town. That's not his card. It's his subsidiary manager's card. Those people, I swear! If it wasn't for economic reforms, they'd still be at the bottom of the heap."

He mopped the floor vigorously, as if it were possible to obliterate the invisible footsteps the nobody had left.

His wife returned her attention to sorting her money, receipts, and paraphernalia. Finishing that, she flipped the card over to read the other side.

"What! This is my boss's card!"

"No . . . that's impossible—" Yao stopped mopping.

"*Impossible?* This is the company manager's name. This is our company name, our address and phone number. How could I be wrong about that?"

They gazed at each other for a long moment, until she suddenly burst out laughing.

"Stop it! What's so funny, eh? What's so damn funny about anything?" he roared.

"A *no*body! The only thing you're good for is for talking big! I know this guy has a personal fortune worth tens of millions of yuan! You think you're a somebody, but me, your wife, has to run all over the city, playing up to a whole lot of nobodies to get a job so she can make a little more money. And for all that, I get transferred to a subsidiary of your middle-school classmate's company. A subsidiary! And 'Mr. Somebody's' wife is a third-rate employee! And one day, when the boss loses his current interest in your wife, it'll be all over for her. But you—you just sit at home thinking of yourself as a person of quality! *You* . . ."

His wife had worked herself into a feverish pitch, and this was the time to unload. It seemed to her that her stomach had been stuffed with nails for way too long. Now that the time had come, she shot the nails from her mouth directly at her husband. Yao Chun-gang felt as if he were bristling, like a hedgehog. Some of the nails tore through his flesh and struck his heart, leaving it full of holes. He thought that she was even more hateful than Sun Ke, for the pain she was causing him hurt far worse than anything Sun Ke had done.

He threw the mop aside and ferociously slapped her face.

She stopped yelling. She stared at him with one hand pressed against the burning side of her face. Tears streamed down from her eyes while her mouth still formed a sickly smile.

The momentary effect was bizarre, as if the upper and lower parts of her face were formed from two separate halves.

"That's good! You said it all out, you shameless bitch!" He replied to her disjointed smile with a cold smirk of his own. "To get on your fucking boss's good side, you slept with him, didn't you! He was the one who taught you those bedtime acrobatics, wasn't he! And you wanted to try out your new fucking skills on me when you got home, didn't you! You thought he was going to be your *fucking coach*. So what am I, your drill field? I am your legal husband! You think I'm such a fool that I'd never catch on? Well, just remember—I'm in psychological research! You were going to practice on me and get it down so you could *really* service your fucking boss, isn't that it! I ought to strangle you!"

He lost all control and came at her.

She quickly dodged and fled to the bedroom. He chased after her, but she shut him out.

He moved like a caged wolf, pacing breathlessly from the living room to the bedroom door. He pounded and kicked the door, roaring terribly. He grabbed the ashtray in the living room and started to throw it at the TV set but sent it smashing into the floor instead. He collapsed onto the couch and buried his head in his arms, weeping.

After Yao Chun-gang had wept enough, he ran to the bedroom door again, this time begging his wife to open it. He apologized for his madness. He begged her to forgive him. He even slapped his face loudly to punctuate his regret.

"Let's make up. I only said those things to blow off steam. I shouldn't have hit you. I've been working on getting transferred. I'll get myself transferred to a private company where I can be the manager, or assistant manager. I could get at least a thousand yuan a month. Honey, I'm kneeling down to you."

He knelt down outside the door and started to cry all over again. As he leaned against the door, it gave way. It had been unlocked, and she was gone. She had slipped away, and he had not even noticed.

Zhao Jing-yu was taken aback by Yao's appearance when he showed up at his office the next morning.

"What happened to your eyes?"

"Oh, nothing, really. They were a little itchy yesterday evening, and when I woke up this morning, they were red and swollen."

"It isn't pinkeye, is it?"

"No, it couldn't be that."

"I think it is. They look too red. How's your foot?"

"Much better. I can wear shoes now."

"How's the joints in your neck now? You go see a doctor?"

"Not yet. I'm doing therapy at home."

"Look—you're sick all over. Why are you coming in to work now? You should pay more attention to your health."

"Yes, I should. I came in to take care of that business for Comrade Qu."

"Yes, of course. Your wife called me about it. I've thought it over again. Let's do her this one favor. Here is the contract. I give you full authority to sign this contract with her, and I won't question it anymore."

Zhao Jing-yu dug the contract out of his papers but bypassed Yao's outstretched hand. Instead he lay the document on his desk and pinned it under his own, large hand.

"But," he continued, "there is one condition. One thing we have to agree on. Know why I turned you down the first time? I'd already decided that Miss Zhang was going to set up the same kind of project. I'd already talked it over with her. Of course, she was very enthusiastic. Then the phone call I got from your wife threw me into a dilemma. I've always respected your wife's feelings, so I promised her I'd take care of it right away. But how do I explain this to Miss Zhang? I thought about this the whole night. Now I've decided to solve the problem this way: let's promote Miss Zhang to be vice director. That will smooth her feathers back down. Besides, research institutes like ours usually have one executive director and two vice directors. With one director and only one assistant, our management team actually is substandard. With Miss Zhang working as vice director, it'll take some of the load off your shoulders, too. Nowadays they're encouraging us to promote young people. We should go along with the reforms, don't you think? With Miss Zhang in place, our management team will have the perfect combination of old, middle, and young."

Finishing his speech, Zhao Jing-yu looked Yao straight in the eyes to watch carefully while awaiting the expected answer.

"I agree."

Zhao Jing-yu smiled.

Yao smiled, too.

"I knew you would agree."

Zhao Jing-yu withdrew his hand from the contract. Yao picked it up off the desk.

Zhao Jing-yu continued. "Miss Zhang is a capable girl. She's reliable and disciplined in her work. We should take good care of her."

Yao did not reply but folded the contract and turned to go.

"Chun-gang, from now on, you just take care of the attendance, meetings, and the general institute affairs. It makes me feel guilty to see you so worn out."

Yao stopped at the door. He understood what Fat Zhao was

telling him. From now on he was vice director pretty much in name only. There could no longer be any doubt about it: He was no match for shrewd old Zhao Jing-yu. He would never win against Zhao.

He turned to look at Zhao Jing-yu, and said, "Thanks . . . a lot."

Out in the hallway, he saw Young Zhang approaching from the opposite direction. Noticing him in front of her, she hesitated for an instant before ducking into the lady's room.

He passed the lady's room door but did not go downstairs. Instead he lit a cigarette and smoked, leaning against the wall.

After a moment Young Zhang came out of the lady's room and proceeded toward the director's office. He coughed loudly behind her. Startled, Young Zhang quickly looked around. She blushed to find that he was still there. She stood speechless, completely flustered.

Yao smiled delightedly. "Go ahead," he said, imparting as much significance as possible. "Old Zhao is waiting for you now. He wants to give you some news. You'll be jumping up and down!"

THE ADDRESS WAS a high-rise in the suburbs, but not too far out of town. Nice environment, too, Yao noticed: watered lawns everywhere. The neighborhood streets were clean and orderly. It was the perfect place for people who appreciate tranquility.

"Come on in." The rabbit-faced woman opened the door and stepped aside to let him enter. She gave him a welcoming smile. The door had a peephole, and he assumed she had checked to see who was there before opening the door. He saw that she had a brand-new burglarproof door. The decorative pattern of the iron bars added a disguise of graciousness.

Yao had called her on the phone before leaving the institute, and happened to catch her at home.

"Are you going to be home today?" he had asked.

"Yes, I don't feel like going out today."

"Okay. Well, I want to come over to your place right away."

She seemed hesitant, unable to say yes or no.

"*Okay? . . .*" The tone of supplication in his voice was that of a child begging his parent.

She laughed ambivalently, a woman's laugh that told him she knew exactly why he wanted to come over.

"I've got the contract and I'll bring it with me."

"*Really?*" There was a tinge of derision to her voice.

"It's true!" He was worried that she didn't believe him.

"Okay . . if that's what you want to do."

"I'll be there right away. Hey . . . you don't have anybody else there, do you?"

"Yes, I do."

He did not know what to say.

"I was only kidding," she said. "I'll be waiting for you."

She gave him directions to her flat, and added, "Go ahead and take a cab. I'll pay for it."

He would have taken a cab even if she hadn't suggested it. His thirst for her was as intense as a baby's on its first whole day of weaning; he cries piteously and stretches out his hands to clutch something—a baby bottle or his mother's breast.

Naturally he didn't give her the taxi receipt.

"Give me the receipt," she said, "before I forget about it."

He shook his head resolutely, as if her paying the fare would be an unacceptable affront. "How could I have you pay for the taxi? This is business. The institute will pay for it. I'm a vice director: why wouldn't they cover my taxi fare?"

She didn't persist. "It's up to you." She smiled again.

It was hot outside, at least 35°C, but the air-conditioning kept her apartment quite cool. She was wearing a knee-length scarlet nightgown with a low, embroidered neckline. The whole thing was held up by two spaghetti straps and was almost completely open in the back. He could plainly see she wasn't wearing a bra. Her pert, white breasts seemed to be expanding through the embroidery, like two snow-white steamed rolls in a red knit bag.

"Would you like to see my apartment?"

His gaze was still fixed on her breasts. He nodded with self-constraint. She started showing him around her four-bedroom unit. She had decorated each room in a different style, the overall effect being an array of colors in wallpaper, carpeting, and furniture. In her bedroom he saw crowds of dolls big and small, Western and Oriental, which created the appearance of a little girl's room. Upon the walls, however, she had hung up pictures of Chinese and foreign male movie stars—and alongside them, enlarged and half-nude or completely nude photos of herself, all obviously taken in this bedroom. With pictures of herself amongst the movie stars, she looked like a star, too—a seductive movie star; all the poses in her pictures were patently alluring.

He attempted a quick mental audit of what it must have cost her to furnish the place and guessed, *At least thirty thousand . . . No—more than that!*

"We don't have to go back to the living room. We're not strangers," she said. "The living room air conditioner makes it too cold for me." Before he could say anything, she sat down cross-legged on the carpet, her lingerie drawn up to her thighs. The scarlet fabric drawn over such white skin dazzled his eyes.

"Sure," he said, and sat down on the floor, too.

"Want a drink?"

"No . . ."

"Let me get you something."

There was a small refrigerator in the bedroom. She opened the door and took out a bottle and two chilled champagne flutes.

"White wine. It's low-alcohol. I really love it." She filled the two glasses.

"Your home is pretty elegant." He took a sip of wine while he tried to think of something to talk about.

"It's so-so. Just a place to live. They only have condos here, no work-unit housing. Way too expensive for regular people. I moved in three months ago. This high rise is still only half full. Won't be full for another three to five years. It's mostly vacant, and that's the way I want it. Nobody knows anyone else. Nobody bothers anyone else. It's perfect. My guests stop by and leave, and never worry about what somebody is going to think. It's out of the way to get here, but that's okay. I have a car. I drive wherever I want to go. It doesn't seem inconvenient to me."

"You mean . . . you have a car?" he asked like a simpleton.

She smiled sympathetically.

"What's so strange about me driving a car? It's not a very good one. A Santana. I'll keep it for a couple of years. I was seriously thinking about leaving the country last year. But I've changed my mind since then. Life's not bad here."

She raised her glass and drank down the wine. She squinted at him briefly before changing the subject. "So, you're what—forty?"

"Forty-five." He seemed embarrassed to say so, as if being forty-five was something a man ought to be ashamed of.

"No. You look at least seven or eight years younger than that. Refined in your manners, too. I'm partial to the intellectual type." She smiled again, seductively.

"You see? I did bring this!" Her bed seemed to beckon him, and his thoughts were elsewhere, yet he found himself talking about the contract. He had no choice but to hand it over to her.

She gave it a quick look before setting it aside casually on the carpet.

"Well, I don't need this anymore," she said. "I went with another business unit. I was in a real bind. I had to cut a deal as fast as possible because I stood to make two hundred thousand yuan. But I would never have been able to close the deal if they knew all I had was a clothing shop. I needed a much bigger image. Anyway, it went through, and they've deposited two hundred thirty thousand yuan into my account. If I can make one more deal like that before the end of the year, I'm going to call it quits. I just don't want to run a business anymore. I'm tired of it. I had to go all the way over to your institute ten times, plus all the other places I had to go to. Your director, Zhao, was so mean to me. I'll bet he came out of the army, didn't he? I really do not like grouchy old men. If I had gone along with what he wanted my third trip there, I could have had everything signed and sealed. That was my mistake. . . ."

She spoke glibly, frankly, as if she were confiding to her closest, most trusted friend. Her voice was languid and soft. The effect it had on him was irresistible.

"I . . ." He grabbed her hand. As if in a mirage she had become a big, white, tender steamed roll, the type that country people cooked for spring festival. In his delirium, her scarlet skirt became the edible red seals they used to decorate their dim-sum treats. He felt so hungry that his heart was racing.

She withdrew her hand.

"I almost forgot. I've got something for you, too. My memory is so bad. Before I forget . . ."

She stood up and stepped lightly out of the room. She returned, holding two bundles of banknotes.

"This is yours." She tossed the notes onto the carpet. The wool was so thick that the money dropped with scarcely a whisper.

"Two thousand. Hope you don't think it's too little. I got it together right after you called. The contract you brought over is no use to me anymore, but I know you worked hard on getting it for me. Here's my appreciation."

She sat down on the carpet and crossed her legs in front of him again, only this time much closer. He thought he could already smell the fresh scent of the female body.

"Don't you feel hot at all? You can take your clothes off. After all, we're not strangers. And don't worry. Nobody's going to come by."

She smiled, making him dizzy. He pounced on her and pressed her down onto the carpet.

"Don't be so impatient." She giggled. "You like the carpet better than the bed? Greedy cat!"

But by then he had lost all self-restraint. He wasted no time in moving to the bed. His desire to have her had transformed him into a wildcat that had just found a fresh fish. He not only had to have her body, he wanted to have her four-bedroom elegant apartment, her huge bank account, her clothing shop. The first forty-five years of his life now seemed like a miserable joke, and he would trade it all to marry her and possess everything she owned at once.

He continued to kiss her while he shook off his pants. In the process he kicked over the loosely bundled two thousand yuan.

"I want to marry you! Oh, I want to marry you!"

"You idiot! You forget you have a wife?"

"I'll divorce her! I will divorce her!"

Again she giggled.

"You guys are so funny. You intellectuals—you come up with the weirdest ideas. Marry me? Whatever put that idea in your head? What would I need a husband like you for? Listen here—I would never marry you. When we're both in the mood, we'll just enjoy ourselves. What's the difference?"

She rubbed his nose with her little finger.

"No, that would be different! Different!"

However, his erection, which had filled him with so much confidence a moment before, shrank away upon hearing her words. No matter how he tried, there was no bringing it back to life.

"Look at you! You're not even any good in *that* department! How could you think you could marry a woman like me? I expect the best, whether I'm making money or making love. Think you could satisfy me?"

She rubbed his nose again sympathetically. Then she heaved a sigh of displeasure with his penis and its uselessness, at least for the time being.

He began to sob desperately as he lay on her body.

"Come on, now. Don't cry. Be a good boy."

She was not disappointed. Actually, she was rather amused.

Deaf

THE DAY BEGAN without a hint that anything unusual could happen.

The weather was quite pleasant. I remember looking out of the window and seeing a crystal-clear sky filled with sunlit brilliance. It was a gorgeous, altogether fantastic view of the universe.

I was entirely normal myself. No—that is completely incorrect. What I mean is I believed, or, looking back in retrospect, I *thought* I was entirely normal.

Stay with me and you'll see that I'm a person who is right just about every single time.

You also have to understand that I'm a creature of habit. I always sit down to eat after I've washed up. I don't wait until after I've eaten, like those characters who aren't so fastidious. And, of course, I sit up straight while eating—further proof of my discriminating nature.

From the day I first used chopsticks, they have been in my right hand, the way normal people do in conformance with the rules. Not even on that very first day did I take it into my head to go against the rules. I sat on the chair and placed the bowl squarely on the table; the idea of sitting on the table and placing the bowl on my chair would never have occurred to me.

Anyhow, the day it began, I recall looking up and seeing the big, picture calendar that hangs on the wall. The movie star in the picture looked quite sober—simulating "deep think," as they say. Nothing peculiar about her, either. She wasn't casting seductive eyes at me, and her lovable, staged, deep think didn't leap out of the picture, either.

I had been having gastric troubles, which kept me from eating too much. However, I had also had a bout with hepatitis, which required that I take more nutritious foods. Well, how was I to solve this contradiction? I did not review Mao's dialectics. Neither did I take up *qigong* or go on traditional herbal medicines. What I did was focus on that month's picture on the calendar while I ate. I'd take a bite of food and a glance at the picture, every day at every meal. You surely have heard "Fresh, delicate looks from a beauty sharpen the appetite." I can tell you it's not just an old saying. It is scientific fact. I know this because I used to have one bowl of rice gruel for breakfast. However, by gazing at the flowering beauties on the wall, I could finish two bowls of rice gruel—didn't need any spicy appetizers or pickles or anything else! I obtained the best results during June, July, and August—movie stars wear such skimpy outfits in the summer. Just seeing them would cool and caress me to the bottom of my heart.

My wife had gone to work, my son to school. The TV was on.

A girl wearing a snug-fitting, red, traditional-style dress was singing into the microphone that she clutched. Her slender body undulated as if she were performing for an Indian snake charmer. She was singing the song "Life and Death" for all she was worth.

The misfortune struck just as I was returning my eyes from the TV screen to the picture calendar.

Bang!

My dear readers! Although I have tried to depict that sound in a word—*b-a-n-g-!*—I would have to say now that, actually, it was more of a . . .

But, then, no; it wasn't a gunshot. How could gunfire intrude upon the crystal-clear sunlit brilliance of a gorgeous, altogether fantastic view of the universe? Anyway, the sound wasn't precisely like a gunshot.

At the same instant, my porcelain bowl full of rice gruel dashed against the concrete floor. The blue-and-white china shattered. Gruel splashed everywhere. Although I have written down the sound as a *b-a-n-g*, nothing at all like that accompanied the disintegration of my breakfast bowl; had there been a *b-a-n-g* or a *c-r-a-s-h*, the event and the morning would have been perfectly normal, and I would have gone on singing praises to life as sweet as honey.

However, I did not hear the rice bowl crash.

The bowl fell through the air silently. It came apart silently. I gazed down upon the fragments as if in a trance. Suddenly, it occurred to me that there must be something terribly wrong with the bowl, something possibly even evil.

How could it shatter silently?

A bowl—fine china, no less—shatters on the concrete floor without a sound! Now wouldn't that be more startling than the same event accompanied with the normal *c-r-a-s-h*?

If I am anything, I am sedulous. I rather expect you've figured that out by now. I took out another bowl of the same exact type. I positioned it high above my head, then cast it fiercely down upon the concrete floor.

I wanted to see for myself if there was something wrong

with me, or something wrong with the silently shattering bowls. On a normal morning like this, such events demanded explanation. Indeed, the entire situation had become so bizarre that my method of investigation was not in any way absurd.

My dear readers . . . if only I could truthfully tell you, *Yes, I did hear the silvery, clear* c-r-a-s-h!

Hapless wretch am I: I heard nothing.

I could see that the situation was growing serious. How, oh, how could that perfect morning become so abnormal? How could this world suddenly turn so abnormal?

Well, it's not as if most people don't suppose that the rest of the world is wrong before pressing on to examine themselves. That morning the entire world seemed to have become profoundly quiet. What physical laws could enable the world do that?

I went over to the TV to adjust the volume. I turned it all the way up. Still not a sound came out. Again I studied the screen. The woman in the tight, red, traditional dress was still singing her heart out, still swaying her slim waist like a charmed snake, but the song hardly affected me. *Song? Sound?* Damn it, I wasn't hearing anything! This was more silent than a silent movie.

Suddenly our neighbor Young Liu appeared in front of me. He was snarling. From the way he was waving his hands, it was obvious that he had gone out of his mind.

The thought still had not occurred to me that the malfunction currently upsetting the world was limited to me! How could I have known that Young Liu had come back home after working the night shift and got jarred awake by my TV? I didn't even stop to ask myself how he got into my apartment without making a sound, let alone why I didn't hear what he said even though he was barking forcefully at me. I must admit that one can get so caught up in everyday life that when abnormality intrudes it can seize us unaware and dumbfounded.

I thought it might help settle the situation if I asked Young Liu for some advice. "What do you think could be wrong with my TV set? The picture is okay, but there's no sound coming out."

The young man began to gesticulate like a deranged mime. He came right up to my face and formed some words with his lips. Then he flicked out an index finger, fiercely jabbed the TV's power button, and stomped out of my apartment.

The door shut abruptly behind him. I saw it clearly enough: the door closed powerfully in front of me without a whisper of sound.

This suddenly strange world was really confusing me. I was still completely unprepared to understand what was happening. I slumped into a chair, my thoughts all a muddle. After a long moment, I suddenly awoke to the truth: *I've lost my damn hearing! I've gone deaf! What in the hell is going on?*

The day before, I had been extremely normal. I heard everything. Before I fell asleep, my wife gave me a kick and said, "Get back over on *your* side! You're pushing your son and me out of bed." And then my son said to me, "Hey, Dad—scratch an itch for me. On my back. Right here."

I remembered it all quite clearly. It wasn't a dream.

My . . . misfortune, then, started in the morning.

I was forced to ask myself, *Am I, indeed, deaf?*

So, is the rest of the world still perfectly normal? Is there nothing wrong with *it*?

So, the silence of the two shattering bowls did not involve preternatural craftsmanship.

So, I don't have to send the TV to the repair shop.

So . . . I guess it was my fault the neighbor got overexcited.

No! I thought, *I don't buy any of it!* I simply was unable to believe that I had gone deaf!

I leaped to my feet and shouted at the top of my voice, "O-o-o—ho ho ho!" the way hill people call to villagers over on the next mountain.

Shit! I couldn't even hear my own shouting. My voice seemed to evaporate right out of my mouth. When you can't hear yourself yelling, my dear readers—just put yourself in my position; think how strange it would make you feel!

My apartment door opened again. The little girl from a few doors down the hall poked her head in and looked at me with wide eyes. As soon as she saw me looking back at her, she ducked out and ran away.

I noticed the wall between my apartment and Young Liu's suddenly begin to shake. Since the wall is paper thin, I could guess that the man was mightily pounding on it. A shell mosaic we had on that wall fell to the floor. It shattered in the same bizarre way the china bowls did.

This is too damned much! I thought to myself. I wasn't referring to Young Liu, either. How could the world be like this? Every doomed object around would crash in silence to me from now on. My dear readers, just imagine what I had to look forward to. A thief comes in and noisily ransacks the cabinets and drawers, and I don't even know it's going on unless I see him. Suppose I forget to turn off the gas range in time and the pressure cooker blows a hole through the ceiling; I'd have to figure out what happened by looking through the mess. Going deaf has to be stranger than just being blind. At least a blind person could hear the thing go off, and then they would *know* what happened. You would have to agree that sound is what makes this world vibrant and meaningful. A completely silent world, a world without a single sound, would be nothing but a series of cartoons. Everything becomes unreal, and that includes your own existence. Nothing would be the way it is when you are whole.

Filled with confusion and apprehension, I walked to the closet mirror. Of course, I had not visibly turned into a monster. Actually, I looked more decent than usual: My hair, which I part in the center—some people call it the "young Mao" look—was still blow-dried and sprayed; the dark gray suit made me look experienced and prudent; the tie with diagonal red-and-black stripes was knotted properly—not too tight, not too loose—about my perfect neck—not too thick, not too thin. My Adam's apple was not too high up, and the skin on my neck looked clean, too (not all men's necks do look clean, you know), rather like a wooden stake with a ball on top, and IQ enough inside. The face: plain and square, and if read through would yield but one word: pleased. I had tidied this face up myself. It was shaved by an imported razor blade that cost me almost one yuan. And yet all of this had lost its meaning for me.

It was supposed to have been one of the most important days of my life. The day before, I had been appointed executive director of the Literature and Fine Arts Development Trust and Research Institute—a chief bureau-level position! I was scheduled to deliver my inaugural speech to my subordinates. But in the morning, I lose my hearing! I'm deaf! I had been dreaming of getting this promotion for the previous three years, four months, and twenty-seven days. And, if I did the math correctly, I got the position more than two thousand days ahead of my own plan. My predecessor had caught a fatal disease and died quickly, to my good fortune.

But! . . .

How could the director of the Literature and Fine Arts Development Trust and Research Institute be deaf!

Oh, Blessed Mother Mary!

I sank into the chair and began to ponder.

One who is blind cannot disguise his blindness, neither can a cripple escape public notice. Have a cold? Then you will sneeze and have a runny nose. Have a high fever and you are sure to shiver or even become delirious. Deafness, though, is a different story. Nobody can detect it just by looking at you. Then it came to me: *If I don't tell anyone, who will know I'm deaf? So, why tell anyone?*

Thinking about it that way restored some hopefulness to me about my life and my career.

What is so bad about being deaf, anyway? All right: I can't hear anything. What's so bad about not being able to hear anything? How many times have we all wished we could have just one minute of tranquility free from the noisy distractions that surround us?

So then and there I pulled myself together. I took out a Walkman and put on the headset. And I put on a reserved smile like one of those successful, satisfied, middle-aged people who go out and survey the world from their superior position—and I went out. I felt positively indomitable. Chairman Mao's words rang in my ears: "Be determined. Fear no death. Surmount difficulties and win victory!"

The essential thing about tranquility is that it reminds us from time to time how untranquil the world is; I'll get back to that in a moment.

People who are born deaf cannot imagine what it is like to hear, just as people who are born blind cannot fathom the concept of color. However, as my dear readers know, my case is entirely different because I became deaf only a short while ago. Nevertheless, the sensation I—a person of acquired deafness—

experienced when I stepped outside onto the pavement was positively surreal.

All kinds of vehicles moved through the street's traffic lanes *silently*. Pedestrians silently walked this way and that.

A gardener clipping his ornamental shrubs caught my eye, and I stopped to watch. The half-meter-long shears snipped away without a single sound. The twigs tumbled down without a sound. At the halfway point, the gardener paused and took out a hammer from his tool bag. Then I saw him lay the shears out on the curbstone and hammer on them. To me this was no more than a series of silent movements. The gardener noticed that I was watching him and gave me a frosty stare. Then he said something. Of course, I don't know what he said, but I did not want the first man I met that day to figure out I was deaf. Wishing to appear normal and say something appropriate, I looked up at the sky and answered, "What weather!" and chuckled politely.

The man stood up and came over to me. He took out a pack of cigarettes and shook one loose, then pulled it out with his lips.

Thinking he was probably asking me for a light, I quickly drew out my lighter and offered it to him. He lit up with his own lighter and drew the first puff or two. Staring sternly into my face, he said something again

I was getting confused.

Supposing that I was expected to say something in return, I said, "I would very much like to help you, but could you please make your words clearer?"

He squinted at me. Then he snatched my headset, bent it around my neck, and roared something into my left ear.

From the exaggerated working of his lips, I was almost

certain that what he said was, *"Go to hell!"* I noticed that passersby had stopped and gathered round, obviously attracted by the prospect of seeing something happen. Realizing that my situation was becoming unfavorable, I turned to leave.

But he wouldn't let me go. He grabbed me by my lapels. I bucked up, and said loudly to him and all present, "Sir, a gentleman uses his tongue, not his fists! You all saw what happened: I never touched him, but he's going to use his fists. Well, I'm an intellectual! We know how to control ourselves. I never did anything to offend him. . . ."

He had been talking to the crowd at the same time, in a rather cocky way if I may say so. Needless to say, I didn't get a word of what he said. Worse, I could see that he was winning the masses over to his side because the men and women quieted down and were giving me accusing looks.

Feeling that my position was getting desperate, I blurted out, "I am deaf!"

The men and women all laughed out loud. To me, all was calm, absolutely quiet. How I wished that dialogue balloons would drop down so we could all see what everyone was saying. That way, these nosy people wouldn't be laughing at me, and I myself would know what was going on between me and the gardener . . . and why he was so angry, as if I could have humiliated him grievously enough to warrant such mistreatment.

The men and women laughed for a while, getting some kind of satisfaction out of the way things went, and then began to disperse. This left the gardener and me alone again.

He let go of my suit coat and then burst out laughing, too. He straightened up my tie and positioned my headset back in place over my ears. He tapped me on the shoulder, grumbled something or other, and then went back to work.

I rushed away without daring to look back. If I hadn't been

dressed like a respectable intellectual, I would have made a flat-out run for it. I got to a bus stop and waited, still quite bewildered about whatever had just happened.

I noticed that across the street a store was having a grand-opening celebration. The store gate was flanked by a band of a dozen people energetically playing some music. A whole braid of firecrackers went off, filling the air with the smell of gunpowder.

Suddenly, the men and women around me started to scatter. I looked down to see a fizzing M-80 skittering right up to my shoes. With eyes wide open, I watched the thing explode, immediately yielding a big hole in its smoking center.

I stood there not blinking an eye. The other men and women, their hands still clapped over their ears, watched me in amazement, as if I were not a man but a robot. All of a sudden, I felt kind of proud. Compared to them, I was something special. I may have become deaf, but I had something on these people. I felt certain that this kind of advantage would come to me often.

I even mused that being deaf might not be such a misfortune. The world had turned interesting in a way, full of wit and humor that was really enjoyable. I could have a lot of fun. Why, wasn't I myself full of wit and humor, too? Now I could appreciate life even more.

A bus pulled up silently at the curb. People silently pushed their way aboard. I inadvertently stepped on a young man's foot. He cussed me out silently—I was pretty sure from his facial expressions that he was doing more than just informing me that I had stepped on his foot—and then he hit me in the chest. While doing that, he stepped on a woman's toes. She screamed silently and smacked him a good one with her handbag. Well, he was not about to let her get away with that. They escalated into such a raging battle of words that they forgot about getting on the bus. The doors closed silently against my back, right after I squeezed aboard. The bus conductor picked up the public-address microphone and said something. As the bus pulled away, the young man and the woman were still hurling insults silently.

I noticed how much this was like living in a vacuum contained in a jar. Another idea flashed through my mind: Deafness could be a wonderful advantage for brain workers such as philosophers, novelists, and poets — people who are always complaining they can't find the solitude they need to ponder their deep thoughts. If someone could invent a chemical treatment or even surgery to induce deafness, then all civilization would benefit from such people's heightened productivity!

A man standing beside me gave me a nudge and mysteriously tucked a folded slip of paper in my hand. He looked like he was from some other part of China. I opened the paper and read: *Dear Comrade: I am deaf. Could you please tell me on this paper how to get to Royal Lane? Thank you.*

I looked at him. He was smiling at me modestly and trustfully.

Well, if he was deaf, no point in wasting time talking to him. I took out my pen from my suit-coat pocket and started writing on the bus conductor's cramped counter: *Which one do you want? Old Royal Lane or New?*

He took my pen and wrote: *I didn't know they had Old and New Royal Lanes.*

So I wrote: *Old Royal Lane is the first crossroad on Old Culture St. Old Culture St. is near Civilization Square. Get off at Democracy Alley and transfer to the Liberty Ave. trolley. But — Old Royal Lane has been condemned. They're going to tear it all down. New Royal Lane is at the end of Government Ave. Turn left. Take another left—keep turning left, 4 or 5 turns, then ask for New Royal. Are you looking for a commercial or residential unit?*

The paper was full of my jammed-together characters.

The deaf man took the pen from me again and turned the paper over. He wrote: *I am looking for an old* qigong *specialist they say can cure deafness.*

I wrote: *I remember reading in the paper about an old* qigong *practitioner who specialized in deafness. But he died. Cancer of the middle ear. You may want to check with the evening newspaper office for details. Three stops from here, on your left.*

A look of disappointment swept over the man's face. He put away the paper and shook my hand gratefully.

The bus conductor was looking at me respectfully, too, as if in her eyes the model of the selfless Socialist Lei Feng had come back to life and was helping people in distress all over again.

Then a strange thought came into my head: *What if all at once everyone went deaf?* You would have to expect everyone eventually to forget about communicating through speech, like a discarded habit. People would have to rely on pen and paper. Nobody would be trying to talk to me, and I wouldn't have to worry about being exposed as a deaf person. Look at what just happened: thanks to that deaf man there, I—at least as far as everyone else on the bus knew—I wasn't deaf. I could see the congratulations in their smiles when they looked at me.

Well, all right then: one . . . two . . . three . . . go! Now, if I could turn them all deaf, just like that, that is, if all of them crossed over the hearing/deaf line, then the only normal person would be—me!

One . . . two . . . three . . . go!

But the world was silent. Absolutely silent. A silent bus . . . and I was the only one engaged in deficient thinking—me with my Lei Feng trustworthy, ready-to-jump-in-and-help smile as acknowledgment for all those adulatory looks cast at me.

The bus lurched violently as if it were a horse cart and the old jade had just given it a kick. We had hit a big truck.

The traffic police showed up.

A lot of people wandered over to gawk at the wreckage.

A police car with a blinking eye on top arrived.

The bus door opened. The conductor yelled over the passengers' heads, silently.

All the men and women and children quietly got out of the bus, some exclaiming silently.

The two deaf men filed out; one anxious about not being understood, the other anxious about being discovered.

I saw people in the crowd gloating over the accident. I saw passengers gloating over the mess also.

I would never understand the second group. What in the hell kind of satisfaction could they get out of a wreck on the bus they were riding in?

The deaf man shook my hand again and mouthed a lot of words. He wasn't in a hurry to go away.

Maybe we are too ready to take offense from one another. Just be a little civil to someone, and he's overwhelmed by the honor you've paid him. As I, the local deaf resident, watched the retreating figure of the out-of-town deaf man, I suddenly felt as if I had ignored something important; it was as if another ship had sailed past me in the night and I had missed it.

WHEN I GOT to the institute, Old Zhang, the security guard, stepped out of the reception office and handed me some newspapers. He talked on and on very respectfully about something. His lips moved up and down. Then I noticed that he hesitated. From this I surmised that he was asking me to consider replacing him with his younger daughter after he retired from the institute.

I answered, "Of course; don't worry. I know about your situation, even though you haven't talked to me about it. But I'll need some time to think things over. These matters require some time for consideration, don't you think?"

Actually, Old Zhang was not the only one at the institute hoping to pass his job along to one of his children. We had at least a dozen of them. It would not be easy to settle them all. Take Old Zhang: if we considered the applicants strictly according to their abilities, he and his daughter would be the very last ones. When I said, "These matters require some time for consideration," it was only a strategy, of course; all of the previous directors had used it. I guessed I'd be using it a lot.

When he heard what I said, Old Zhang looked dumbstruck for a moment. He blinked once or twice but didn't say anything. The only sense I could make of it was that he must have been deeply moved by my words.

Not wanting to get bogged down in something sticky, I patted him on the shoulder and quickly turned away.

I walked into the conference room and found all the department heads and section chiefs already seated, awaiting my arrival. Some whispered silently to each other. Others were spouting their opinions—also silently—. They all stopped talking and straightened up when they saw me walk in. The mood turned solemn.

After I was settled in my chair, I took off the headset, pulled the Walkman out of my pocket, and gently laid the apparatus down on the table. That had them all focusing in on the small stuff—just as if I'd called this meeting to go over quality assessment or the marketing plan for tape players and headsets. My gambit had worked perfectly: I had their attention, and the sound equipment ruled out any stray idea that I could be . . . deaf.

"Comrades," I began, "first of all, let me apologize for arriving twenty minutes late. And why was I late for work today? Well, as I rode on the bus I noticed a man from some other province who was having difficulties because he had lost his hearing. That is to say, he was totally deaf. Well, to make a long story short, the man was writing notes on an old envelope, trying to get people on the bus to give him directions the only way he could hope to understand—with paper and pen. Not a single person would bother to help him. Comrades, we are all aware of the general decline of moral behavior in our society. People don't care about each other anymore. I was so saddened by the experience. But I'll say this: I would rather be twenty minutes late and keep all of you waiting for me than ignore that deaf gentleman's plea for help. Only then would I be able to feel right about coming in to work at all! Well, comrades, you tell me. Am I right, or am I wrong?"

People all around were nodding their approval to each other.

"Comrades, we are a research institute for a cultural trust and its development. Culture is our elder sister: arm in arm she embraces arts on the left and civilization on the right. Comrades, the work we are doing is a glorious mission that history has bestowed upon us! Let us solemnly rise to accept the challenge! The reason why I explained to you about my being late for work today was not because I wished to showcase my conduct; it is because I intend to ask all of our comrades *each one* to become a living Lei Feng, and from this point on to put Lei's glorious example into action. . . ."

My words were overcome by gusts of warm, silent applause. Even though I couldn't hear anything, I knew enough to pretend that I heard everything, as anyone normally would. My behavior seemed completely appropriate.

I could not be certain that every one of them was sincere in the applause. The key point, I guess, was not whether they were sincere, but that I won the applause. It didn't matter whether I actually heard it, either, although I have to admit that silent applause is disappointing. Well, even if they weren't applauding in their hearts, at least they were afraid of me; they wanted to kiss up to me . . . to please me. It's pretty impressive, really—certainly a feeling you don't get from your subordinates day in and day out. It didn't even matter whether or not I could hold them in awe for long. I thought I could last three, four, maybe five years. That wouldn't be asking too much. I'm not an unreasonable person.

As soon as the applause began to subside I continued. "Comrades, everyone of us should institute a regimen of self-examination. Have the courage to analyze and dissect ourselves. Personally, I *advocate* the courage to self-examine and self-dissect. Let me set an example for you. If my drawn-out explanation about being late this morning had any selfish motivation, then it was because . . . I wanted to prove before all of you that your new director is not deaf!"

What laughter! Though silent to me, each one of them was laughing from the bottom of his heart. The meeting that had begun so solemnly had turned quite lively.

"I believe I've achieved my goal, wouldn't you say?"

Yet another burst of silent, hearty laughter.

I didn't laugh along with them, however. I knew that the essence of being the humorist is to take the joke seriously. As they enjoyed the joke I surveyed the scene and thought how lovely these comrades were. Their superior seizes the moment to make a joke, and then he reels them in as if his line had hooked their hearts. I wondered why our protocols for evaluating and appointing officers didn't consider the candidate's sense of humor. I felt a twinge of personal responsibility here. It was a good idea. I absolutely must send it on up to the superior personnel department. I would present my idea very seriously, as seriously as when I proved that I was not deaf.

I continued, "Comrades, look here. What's this? It's a headset. Okay, now what's this? It's a radio and a tape cassette player. What's this stuff for? You can get broadcasts. If we make a habit of listening to broadcasts, we'll become involved in the affairs of the nation and the world. It also lets you listen to music without bothering others. It's very important to learn how to appreciate music. It molds our temperament. It exerts a potentially positive influence over all our artistic sensibilities . . . plus our mental state. Of course, I mean good, *healthy* music. Music is the mother of all the arts. We, all of us here, are cultural workers. You tell me—how could a cultural worker know nothing about music? Therefore, I suggest that we appropriate enough money from our cultural concerns fund to buy a Walkman for everyone at the institute."

More applause. This round went on for quite a while. My regret was that I couldn't hear it.

"Oh, and, uh, yeah—just one more thing. We'll get rid of all the deaf comrades!"

Again, laughter from the bottom of their hearts.

Nowadays superiors can hardly get any applause at all, even if they offer their subordinates first this, and then that. Tapping their sense of humor doesn't automatically get the laughs, either. Frankly I never expected to find myself so popular among my subordinates. I swelled up with pride over the success of my first speech and thought, *How adorable they are!*

"Now I would like to hear what you have to say," I continued. "Let's not limit the subject. Go ahead and say what you think, whether it's critical or constructive about the institute. Creative ideas? Suggestions for renovation? Just open it up right here."

It was quiet all around; actually quiet.

Finally someone started talking. Then others joined in. Some of them talked on and on with self-assurance. Some became excited—standing, and sitting down, and then rising again to continue. If I ignored their facial expressions and moving lips, it looked really funny—as if they were trying to hold back impatient bladders—I could just see them rushing on out of the conference room to the toilet, but they stayed on because they were too embarrassed to go ahead and do it. Some paced back and forth endlessly, silently, as if they were grousing to themselves. Some gesticulated wildly, their eyebrows danced up and down. *The ones that go on and on from one thing to another must be saying a whole lot of nothing,* I thought.

For two and a half hours I sat in place pretending to listen. When one is surrounded by silence, profound silence, everything turns into a mime show. It can amuse or even teach important things. In that regard this ensemble's performance was attaining the level of master artists. The overall effect was that a real *me* and a real *they* were functioning separately within a manageably bizarre situation.

So, to affirm that I was indeed whole—as important to myself as to the rest of them—that what they saw and heard was all there was to it, I courageously *and prudently* assumed a role in the day's mime show. I fixed my eyes hard upon each speaker; I know how important it is to gaze at people when they're talking to you. Naturally my reaction to what they said would be of immense significance to them, and I couldn't let them down, so I would nod from time to time. I interjected comments like,

"Right," "Yes, reasonable," and, "Correct," to encourage them. "Go on. Why did you stop? I can tell you have a lot more to say about that." I even demonstrated my excitement: "Let's all give him a round of applause for that!" I would start clapping, and then everyone else followed my lead. Every now and then I turned aside and stressed to the secretary, "Old Zhang's words are quite to the point. He hit the nail on the head. Write all of it down verbatim." Or, "You know, what Old Li just said is really profound. Don't just sit there listening. Write it down!"

To tell the truth, I was nervous at first. I could make one false move and expose the cloven hoof. But, after a few minutes, I saw that no matter what the speaker said, as long as I gazed intently at him, that I persuaded him that I was listening attentively, if I nodded in approval instead of shaking my head, if I inserted something agreeable and put on a focused, contemplative look—then the speaker would be quite pleased. Others in the audience would take their cues from me and contemplate the speaker's words attentively. Don't think that they're all hypocrites or snobs. It's not that way. I discovered something that day that I might never have discovered had I not gone deaf: If someone says something somewhere between smart and stupid, like, "When you are starving, even a little bit of sugar can quiet your hunger," and you're careful to look extremely serious when they're saying it—just nod in approval, throw them a few bones, like, "How true," or, "Right"—you are sure to pick up followers who will ponder along with you, who will nod with you. They are certain even to chew over those words that are not quite smart and not quite stupid, as if they might taste limitless knowledge and philosophy. If you are their boss and you have authority over them, the enjoyment is all the more intense.

It was odd, but I found myself becoming quite the focused

observer after my hearing went. It was just as they say, You lose one thing, you gain something else. As the meeting progressed, I got better, more natural and at ease. Nobody was getting hurt.

By the time it was up to me to pull things together, I announced, "Comrades, I want to thank you all for sharing your excellent views regarding the future of our institute. In the final analysis, there is only one thing I want to stress: every leader has his or her own leadership style. What *I* really can't abide is a bunch of trash talk at work. This isn't a tea house. So now, I am going to lay down my first office regulation: anyone who needs to submit a request or to report anything directly to me—I don't care if it's big or small—please, you must do it in writing. At the very least, this is a good way to skip a lot of empty words. People who don't care much for verbalizing will be brief and to the point with pen and paper, don't you think? I believe that if we all stick to this rule, we'll end up as more skillful writers. I am *not* encouraging more bureaucracy here. On the contrary, this will help us eliminate a lot of *verbal* bureaucracy! If you agree with me, then let's hear your applause.

The people started to applaud.

I said, "Meeting adjourned."

The meeting ended.

I could see that they were satisfied with my inaugural speech, and I knew why: it was because it had been a unique experience. Unique because I was fresh, novel. Most people are drawn to the unique and novel, especially when it stems from their boss.

I sat in my chair in the director's office the entire afternoon drinking, smoking, and reading newspapers. I enjoyed the general solitude. Well, seven or eight subordinates dropped by to pay a visit, but not one of them talked to me. Instead, each politely laid on my desk a piece of paper with a handwritten note and then went away in silence. I didn't speak to any of them, either. Instead, I wrote my response directly on their pieces of paper: *Agreed* or *Whoa—hold it, Comrade* or *Please send this over to Department Head So-and-So* or *Discuss with Section Chief Blah-Blah-Blah.*

The seriousness with which I responded to the department heads and section chiefs had my secretary following my instructions to the *T.* For her part, she was like a little kitten presented to a new master; she didn't know what I was like and was not about to get too close to me. She spent the entire afternoon outside my office arranging and editing her meeting notes, poring over every detail. I almost forgot she existed.

She submitted the finalized meeting minutes to me before the afternoon break. The sense of relief she felt was written all over her.

After I read the first couple of pages I was fit to be tied. Eighty to ninety percent of the speeches were attacks against me! The complaints were all over the board, but the gist of it was that they were skeptical about me, even questioning my qualifications, my intentions, my alleged lack of experience. Astonishingly, there were *my* comments, too—"Good" and "You hit the nail on the head" and "Very profound" and "Correctly stated"—right in there along with the most unfair, blatant, sarcastic criticism imaginable!

Mime show, hah! I had put on a monkey show! All my valiant self-control and calmness had produced no more than the respect for a monkey. I had to tell myself a hundred times, *Now calm down, Comrade Director, calm down. . . . You did very well this morning. . . . All you have to do is stay calm.*

So I lit up a cigarette. After two of them I began to smile again. I called in the secretary and wrote on the first page, right there in front of the secretary: *What a good meeting! This document should be safely filed away.*

As I handed the minutes to her, I smiled cordially and said, "Miss Wang, you did a wonderful job. You should be commended." It was the first time I had opened my mouth that afternoon.

It could have been my cordial smile that encouraged her. She relaxed her *I'm-really-going-to-catch-hell-for-this* attitude somewhat. She took out a piece of carefully folded paper from her pocket. She opened it up and laid it on my desk. I quickly looked it over. It read: *Director, may I have the honor of inviting you to the opera tonight?*

I couldn't think of any reason not to accept, so I wrote below: *My pleasure to escort you on a beautiful evening!*

She then wrote: *I'm so happy. I'll get myself ready and be right back.*

And then I wrote: *I'll be patiently awaiting you.*

When we got to the front entrance downstairs, the institute's chauffeur was waiting for us; and there I was, stuck with a paid-up month's bus pass.

As we drove away, I knew that if she asked me any questions it could lead to disaster. To grab the initiative, I began to regale her with stories from my childhood, my adolescence, young adulthood; how I have longed for a tranquil, relaxed life in retirement, liberated from responsibilities and obligations.

Though twenty-nine and holding a bachelor of arts degree, Miss Wang was single. She had bold, romantic dreams, but they were frustrated by an overcautious disposition. Her eyes twinkled from time to time like those of a naive little girl. It came as a surprise when I noticed her embroidered diagonal neckline, the delicate eardrops, the lightly applied cosmetics, and slight dimples—she was quite a woman. I began to feel perplexed.

With her irresponsible seduction of me in progress, my impulse was to talk about things other than the previous years of my life; but I couldn't—not with the chauffeur listening in.

I took out the paper we had used for our "conversation" earlier and wrote a note on it: *You look so pretty tonight.*

She smiled, blushing with shyness. I was certain I had caught a glimpse of the actual "fresh, delicate looks from a beauty that sharpen the appetite," as the expression goes.

She gingerly took the pen from my hand and wrote: *Now stop teasing me. I'm already an old woman.*

Really? . . .

Dear readers, forgive me, but I will not be commenting on the opera performance. I have to say that opera is not an entertainment for deaf people. For people like myself, watching an opera would be like listening to a circus on the radio. If I hadn't looked at the program, I would never have figured out that it was *The Queen of Spades*, based on Pushkin's work.

Nevertheless, I whispered over to her from time to time, "Beautiful. . . . The music is so beautiful. . . . It almost seems to me as if the voices are holding back the clouds, and the arias are gently falling snowflakes."

She whispered something every now and then. Whatever it was, it came across as sophisticated and knowledgeable, something like, "Listen to the tenor. His range is so wide, he's practically the Chinese Pavarotti."

I bought her something cold to drink during the intermission. While we were there, a woman got into an argument with the young man selling ice cream. Seeing this as yet another chance to prove to my secretary that I definitely was not deaf, I went over to mediate. I spoke directly to both of them: "Hey, young man, take it easy. I've been listening to you, and you have too hot of a temper. And you, lady, you have quite an attitude yourself. Both of you need to just calm down, don't you think?"

It was not until the end-of-intermission bell rang that my secretary took my arm and ended my performance. As she led me away I mumbled on about quarrels being man-made noise, and how I just could not stand these kinds of . . .

When the opera ended, my thoughtful secretary suggested that we go backstage to meet the singers. That was exactly the sort of thing I was hoping for. Our institute is responsible for development and research in establishing trusts in support of the arts. Every writer, poet, artist, and actor falls within the scope of our research. Those people study their artistic disciplines, of course, whereas our institute not only studies the arts, it also studies the people who are involved in the arts. That's all part of our responsibility. Wouldn't it make good sense for me, the director of the research institute, to get to know the performers? They could get to know me and learn about our institutional mission.

Miss Wang and I made our way backstage. She introduced me to the singers as if I were an authority on the theater. They showed me all due respect, talking with me while they removed their makeup. I felt obliged to say something about their performance; otherwise, I might appear too stiff. I began to praise the opera with glowing comments about the singers and the orchestra, tossing out phrases like, "very highly skilled," "the theme is distinctive," "artistic pursuits are healthy"—all those polite formulas. It's the easiest thing to speak in polite formulas, and the niceties go way up in value when they come from the mouth of an "authority." Some of the singers took out their memo books to make quick notes of things I had said.

IT WAS A quarter to eleven when I got home, long past my son's bedtime. My wife was sitting on the couch, obviously just waiting for me to come home. Although that's not exactly right, either, because as soon as I walked in, she threw me a furious stare and then turned her back to me to show she was not about to talk to me.

As a newly deaf person, especially the deaf new director of a research institute, I was just about done in. What a horrendous day! Working deceit on everyone I met in order to prove I wasn't deaf—it wore me out.

I was so tired I didn't even bother to ask why she was mad at me. I just got out of my clothes, collapsed on the bed, and fell right to sleep.

I was awakened abruptly from a dream by the sensation of my ear being twisted; it was my wife. I rubbed my heavy eyelids and looked at the clock: almost midnight.

"*Ouch!* What are you doing?"

"You know what this is for!"

"I don't know anything," I said, "damn it."

I turned away and tried to go back to sleep.

She twisted my ear again.

That did it. "It's midnight. Are you out of your mind?"

She said, "*Think.* What day is today?"

I looked at the calendar. "Friday?"

"No!"

I checked the calendar again. It *was* Friday. So I said, "Okay, what day do *you* think it is?"

"It's my birthday."

"Your birthday? Is that why you're twisting my ear?"

"I cooked up a really big dinner tonight and waited for you," she said. "But you never showed up. Even our son remembered my birthday. But you! *You . . . you . . .*" She started pummeling my chest as if it were a drum.

I grabbed her by the wrists. "Come on. Stop it, Comrade! We are old husband and wife. Don't act like a spoiled child. Is it a gift you wanted? All right! Anything you want, up to a hundred yuan. I'll go buy it tomorrow."

She started biting my hands, and I let loose of her wrists. She was yelling at me vehemently. All I could do was stare back at her dumbfounded. Everything was silent, absolutely silent.

I suddenly recalled that I had gone deaf. "Don't do this to me," I said loudly. "I've gone deaf! There's no point shouting at me!"

She glared at me, like one crow glowering at another. She may even have been thinking about pecking my eyes out.

She raised her hand and swatted my face with a loud *slap!*

Well, I didn't actually hear the slap of her hand—that was my imagination—but it must have been loud because my cheek immediately started to burn.

In a daze I tried to soothe my burning cheek. I could see that she didn't believe my story. She was reacting so fiercely because she thought I was cheating on her. I realized that of course she couldn't accept my explanation: I had just been carrying on a conversation with her. I knew I was deaf, but then— how could I have just now heard her? It didn't even make sense to me. All around, everything was silent, absolutely silent.

I tried again. "Honey, you have to believe me. *I am deaf!* Don't be angry. Don't argue with me, either, because I know it's true. Facts are facts. Facts speak louder than words. Honey, from now on you have to accept it: your husband is deaf. Now, that's not the worst thing in the world, is it? So . . . don't feel sorry for me, just try to . . . restrain yourself."

"*I . . . am . . . not . . . sad . . . at . . . all!*" She spat each word through clenched teeth.

Oh my God! . . . Good heavens! I looked at her, totally unable to speak. My *ears . . . my ears—they . . . they . . . they could hear again!*

I heard a disembodied voice from outside the bedroom. It was cajoling diabolically, like an urban ghost: "Jichang jumped. . . . Tangta jumped, too. . . . They were good. . . . They obeyed me. It's your turn now. I want you to jump. Now!" I recognized the dialogue from that old Japanese sci-fi movie. Then I heard a song: "The wind, it is blow-ing / The horses, they are neigh-ing / The Yellow River's roar-ing on. . . ."

My eight-year-old son appeared in the doorway. He looked from me to my wife, troubled and on the verge of tears.

I was shocked beyond the power of words to describe. It was worse even than the jolt I had this morning when I realized I had gone deaf. I got up out of bed, walked barefoot to the closet mirror, and studied my face in it. I carefully examined both of my ears. There was nothing about them that looked the least bit changed. I flicked the left ear, then the right: they were still firmly attached, not the least bit loose.

I walked over to the nightstand, picked up the colored porcelain ashtray, and slammed it down onto the concrete floor.

Bang!

I was startled by the sound. After hearing nothing for more than fourteen hours, the most ordinary crash *would* seem startling to me. My son finally burst into tears, not from the noise but because of the way I was acting.

Now it was my wife's turn to become shocked and speechless.

"Hey, son . . . there, there, now, be a good boy." I tried to calm him down. "Don't cry. Daddy isn't arguing with Mommy.

Daddy was playing a joke on her. Daddy wanted to show you a magic trick, but it didn't turn out right." I picked him up and carried him to the youth bed to get him to go back to sleep.

My wife started sobbing.

I pretended I didn't notice and made straight for the bed. I thought, *Either I don't do anything or I stick my neck way out. Trying to convince her that now all of a sudden I'm not deaf anymore would be harder than when I tried to make her understand when I was deaf. I would never be able to prove it. She didn't believe me before, and she won't believe me now. And suppose I actually could convince her that I was deaf then but I'm not anymore . . . but then I go deaf again! She would definitely think I was up to some shenanigans.*

I was starting to feel sorry for myself. I had pretended I could hear when I was deaf, I'd pretended I was deaf when I could hear. That was what it had all come down to—pretending. So, if I couldn't hear her crying, and I didn't happen to notice that she was crying, didn't I have every reason not to pay any attention to her? I decided to go back to sleep.

But no! She was not about to let me do that.

She came up to the bed with a piece of paper in her hand and a peremptory question: "*What's this supposed to mean?*"

She was holding the piece of paper with the notes my secretary and I wrote in the car.

I shook my head. "I told you I'm deaf. Can't hear a word you're saying. Better write it down on paper."

She held her baleful gaze on me for quite a while. I could tell that she hated my guts. She went away and brought back a fresh pad of ruled paper. She wrote on the first page: *What kind of relationship are you having with your secretary? I want the truth!*

I took her pen and flipped over to the next page. *Our relationship is revolutionary and comradely. It won't make any difference if you put a knife to my neck. I have nothing to confess.*

Bullshit! The stuff you two wrote down on that piece of paper is proof plain as day. Don't try to mess with me! I say, "Leniency to those who confess their crime, but severity to those who refuse to."

You don't scare me. Words on paper mean nothing.

They mean you were flirting with her.

In your opinion.

You also carried on shamelessly.

Shamelessly? Explain yourself.

Well, you couldn't write down what you were thinking. So you just put in some dots. You knew she'd get it. But I did, too!

That's ridiculous. A person's behavior can't be proved or disproved by dots on a page.

She wrote: *Oh, but it's the truth! Look—see the dots? In novels they always show man-woman hanky-panky with dots. It's obvious that your obscenities went beyond what language could express. . . .*

You just used them yourself. The dots.

She responded: *Well, at a different time. Under totally different circumstances.*

I could slap the shit out of you.

I dare you! Lay one finger on me and I'll go to the institute . . . tell everyone how you really are. Then I'll divorce you. I'll get custody, too.

You've used a few dots again. Think you can steal the horse, but I can't look over the hedge?

She bore down heavily on the paper: *You're the one who screwed up. Don't think you're going to get me to take the blame.*

My dear readers! When a deaf person intends to be normal,

he only needs to know how to perform normally; but when a normal person intends to be deaf, he can't win. A normal person faking deafness cannot come to any good end. I really think it's better to be actually deaf than to take on the guise of deafness. When you're deaf you can't hear all the nonsense. Your opponents are playing their lutes to an ox. But if you're pretending you're deaf, you have to play your lute to the ox just as convincingly, so that everyone believes you're deaf.

As you talk, your words follow your thoughts almost simultaneously; but when you are writing down your words, it's not at all easy to keep pace with your thoughts. I definitely am not one for that mode of communication. It quickly pushed me into a passive role. After the first few rounds, I wanted to scream something like, *Stop it! Honey—I'm not deaf right now. But if I give you an inch, you take a mile. Stop taking advantage of a deaf faker.* I stifled the words. The main item now was to prevent things from getting any worse. This exchange was a battle, though in pen-and-ink. The words sparked when they ground against each other, like swords and sabers rattling. Before long, though, I was exhausted and ceded my ground, while my wife pursued me mercilessly across every inch of every page.

We used up the first pad. She went to get more paper and came back with another one twice as thick. She soaked the nib of the pen in the ink so long that I myself could feel the weight of it when she drew it out, as if she had loaded a machine gun with ten thousand rounds. I looked at the clock: a quarter to three. I groaned to myself that soon I would be ground pork.

What was the use of putting up a last stand when my defeat was already assured? A real hero knows how to retreat from a hopeless situation. The next time it was my volley I neatly printed the characters on the paper: *I confess. I'm guilty. I am condemned.*

My wife answered: *That is nowhere near enough. You have to write a self-criticism of three thousand characters.*

She laid down the pen, tucked all the pages we wrote into a big envelope, and locked it in a drawer. Then she stretched out her body with a yawn and calmed herself down with a sequence of Cosmic Natural *Qigong* before crawling into bed finally satisfied enough to sleep.

I was left at the table to write my self-criticism.

If I had not been made to do so under duress, I would have gone on protesting my innocence. But when I started to examine myself, I began to wonder if my conscience really was clear. In the car, in the theater as I sat next to my secretary, hadn't I felt irresolute? If the car hadn't been a car—if the theater hadn't been a theater—but a private room, a boudoir, or a bed that we were in, continuing my self-examination here, could I have remained ambivalent at the mental level only? And if not, wouldn't it logically follow that I might have done something indecent?

It's like someone who has never stolen anything in his life; yet can he honestly swear that he has never thought about stealing? And even if he is telling the truth, have thoughts ever entered his mind of how lucky he would be to find something valuable lying in the street? Perhaps the wish occurred only in a dream. In any case, if he reclaims the item from the street in deed, the gain is ill gotten; if in a dream, then he is a thief in his subconsciousness. Can he still feel absolutely innocent?

I remembered a story told about the former American president Jimmy Carter. A world-famous journalist once asked him, "Please tell me, Mr. President, what do you think when you see beautiful women?"

The Yankee answered that he thought about all kinds of things. Most of all he thought about having sex with them. I decided I should learn from Mr. Carter. Isn't honesty a fairly respectable quality in people?

Once I had sorted through the issues, I found myself quite the writer. Beginning with a flourish of the pen, I wrote without stopping. My attitude could not have been more devout nor my frame of mind more liberal. My wife had set a quota of three thousand characters, but after three thousand characters I was only halfway done. By the time I finished my self-criticism, I had written over five thousand seven hundred characters; that's ninety percent over quota.

I don't remember what time it was when I got to bed and fell asleep.

THE NEXT MORNING the first thing I saw when I opened my eyes was a woman's face with tear-filled eyes. I was as much frightened as surprised to see my wife all in tears; what—was she going to punish me day and night?

She handed me a note she had prepared. It read:

My poor dearest, I truly believe that you are deaf now. When you were asleep, I slipped the earphones on your head all the way through four of our loudest rock tapes. I used up three new D batteries, but you slept like a dead dog, except for your snoring. How could you have done it if you really weren't deaf? Do you know how much this is going to affect the communication between you and me and our son? Dear God, how can I accept the fact that you've suddenly gone deaf? . . .

Quietly I read the note she had written, as if I were mulling over some playwright's stage directions, while she sat next to me, sniveling and weeping.

The room suddenly lit up. A flash of lightning streaked across the sky. It might have been followed with thunder because she covered her ears with both hands and buried her head in my arms.

The world had become quiet again, absolutely quiet.

I had become deaf again.

After what she had done to me the night before, I couldn't help but enjoy her distress, as if I had found my revenge.

I asked her where our son was.

She answered with pen and paper: *He went to school.*

I asked her if he knew I was deaf.

He might know, and he might not.

I tried to console her to lift her spirits. I told her that being deaf has some incredible advantages. For example, you don't hear thunder, whining, gossip, or rumors. Since praise and criticism will pass right over you, you will be steady, equally indifferent to disgrace and honor. No noise will ever intrude upon pacified ears. Yours will be a peaceful head, a peaceful mind. The only regret is that you lose the enjoyment of music along with all the noise.

You are so selfish—and inconsiderate of me. It could be very inconvenient to try to communicate with a deaf husband.

I told her that we never communicated very well before I went deaf, so we didn't have much to lose on that point. And anyway, conversing on paper could really speed up and refine our penmanship. As the old saying goes, A mishap may become a blessing.

Another lightning bolt flashed outside followed, I assume, by thunder. My wife covered her ears and pushed her head to my chest. The rain was pouring down quietly. I could see hailstones the size of thumbnails pelting the window. Without the distractions of sound, the sight was especially appealing.

Suddenly, my wife got up and hurried to the window. Despite the downpour and the hail, she opened the window and leaned out to look at something in front of our building. She came back drenched and wrote: *A car has been sitting down there beeping its horn for I don't know how long. Is someone waiting to pick you up for work?*

It hit me that I wasn't just another deaf person, I was the director of an institute. I had to set an example for the others by getting to work on time. I jumped out of bed, threw on my clothes, and rushed toward the door.

My wife caught up with me before I could get outside and held up a note for me to read: *Must wash face often, or it will be full of dirt. —Chairman Mao!*

I hesitated for only a second. "There is a reason why I didn't wash. This isn't a question of personal hygiene. It has to do with how I view the world."

I got settled into the car and saw that the driver was frowning. I could tell right away he was unhappy about the long wait. I put on an apologetic smile and mumbled, "Sorry . . . had to stay up all night to work on a report. Didn't even have time to wash my face."

Hearing that, the chauffeur's stern face brightened up. He smiled back at me, seeming satisfied with my explanation.

I had to mumble the same words again when I stepped into my office and met my secretary face-to-face. Whatever she said seemed very understanding, and really touched me. She left immediately and returned shortly with a basin of warm water, as well as a towel, soap, a toothbrush and toothpaste, and a shaving mug that she had obviously just bought from the institute's small commissary.

I began a leisurely washup in my office. She handed me her facial cream and then a small comb just when I wanted them. I had used my wife's toiletries at home, but this was the first time I had ever used any from another woman—a novel opportunity to fully sense the femininity of another woman's personal lotions and things. An amoral desire to possess germinated in my subconscious mind. It was the desire to possess not only the toiletries but also the owner herself.

Watching her silently carry away the wash basin, I thought, *If only I could turn things around with her.* No, I'm not saying she should be deaf; a deaf secretary, no matter how charming, would be ludicrous. What I mean is, if only I was not deaf, and she *were*. If she were, she would have to write down her requests and reports, and I wouldn't have to worry about anyone discovering that I'm deaf. This reminded me of a foreign film called *Mute Slave* about a female slave who couldn't speak: What great good fortune for her master! I could really understand why the hero in the film doted on his beautiful, mute slave. A woman could reach the epitome of charms if she was beautiful and unspeaking.

I was letting my fancy run wild when my secretary came back and handed me a folded note. I opened it. It read:

> *Director: The chauffeur said you stayed up overnight to write a report. It made my heart ache to think of you wearing yourself out. You are still young, and you just took on the leadership position. You really should pay more attention to your health. Good health is an asset in working for the revolution. Please take good care of yourself.*

It was signed by one of the department heads.

The institute changed directors fairly often—sometimes twice a year, sometimes three times in two years—but the chauffeur always stayed the same. He started out as Young Wang. Then they called him Big Wang. Now the young workers were already calling him Old Wang. The department head who sent me the note was buddy-buddy with the chauffeur. Nobody understood how they could be such good friends—they seemed so different in personality and tastes. The chauffeur was always teasing him or being sarcastic; never showed him a bit of respect in public. But the department head never got mad at Old Wang and just shrugged off the abuse. He kept on good terms with the chauffeur, always giving him cigarettes. It wasn't that he needed Old Wang for anything, either. On the contrary, the chauffeur often came to him for help. One thing was clear, though, to everybody: Because of his friendship with the chauffeur, the department head had been the favorite of all the previous directors at the institute. They had all thought very highly of him. People in management call this "curvilinear ingratiation." It works the same way as Western "mistress diplomacy." I was told that the department head's wife was on the homely side; otherwise he would never have had anything to do with the chauffeur.

My secretary came closer to read the note with me. She grinned silently.

I added one line to the message: *Dribs and drabs will all be preserved in my heart.* Then I folded the note back the way it was and told my secretary to return it to the sender.

As she turned to leave, a sudden gust of wind and rain blew in. She rushed over to close the window, knocking over a thermos bottle in the process. The thermos bounced on the concrete floor soundlessly, the inner flask shattering all over the floor in absolute silence.

I knew there had been a *bang* followed instantly by a *foonk* when the thermos liner shattered, but I heard nothing. I stared at my secretary from behind, positively dumbfounded. Now she . . . *she* wasn't hearing anything, either! After closing the window, she turned round to find the accident she had caused and became quite flustered. She picked up the empty metal shell, laid it out of the way over in a corner, and started to sweep up the mess of shattered glass and hot water.

I moved out of the way while observing her suspiciously, wondering if any more evidence would turn up. After she set aside the broom and picked up the mop, I said, "Let me do it." As I mopped I casually asked, "Were you frightened?"

She had calmed down by then, but instead of answering my question, she took earplugs out of her ears. I wondered why I hadn't noticed she was wearing earplugs; still, I wasn't going to risk betraying my own situation just to pry into hers.

From then on I watched her closely when she wasn't paying attention to me, just to see if I could prove one way or another whether she, too, might actually be deaf.

Dear readers, the facts speak for themselves: The deaf can lead! Look at me: I was not only leading, I was doing a very good job of it. I promulgated my new policies as a central feature of my leadership style. It followed logically that I would write down my instructions or check-off the documents submitted to me. Soon my style had become the regular practice of all my subordinates. The institute took on a decidedly silent and solemn character.

The Walkman radios arrived and everybody was given one. Soon, from the front desk to the dining room, to the rest rooms and in every office, almost everyone I saw was wearing a head-set. I wondered what kind of music or radio program they could listen to all day long without getting tired of it. I even began to suspect that this ruse I had worked up for my own protection might actually be shielding other deaf ones among us from being found out. Interestingly, now that my initiative was all the vogue, it didn't matter anymore whether I wore a headset or not.

I thought over the implications. What if the thing we call "spirit" residing deep within our minds turns out to prefer solitude and tranquility? It would be our *personality* that doesn't like to be left alone. One could even suspect that our spirit, in its quest for freedom, could ditch us to gain its own liberation. Another aspect of all this is the wonderfully progressive new mode of behavior among my subordinates: I put them all in headsets and they acted like they had finally found a way to mind their own business. They spent less time on chitchat, boasting, and gossip. The ones who used to love prying into other people's personal affairs, or plot dark strategies behind closed doors, or wage interminable cold war with each other now seemed to care less about such matters. There were fewer favors, fewer frowns; less loathing, less fighting, less friction. They seemed to have discovered a higher stage of security.

I was delighted with this turn of events.

WHEN THE BOMBSHELL hit, it struck me like a bolt out of the clear blue sky. A friend of mine who worked in my parent organization passed secret information along to me: They had received a letter signed by people in my institute denouncing me as a deaf director. The superior took the letter seriously, saying that to let a deaf person try to fill the post of an officer was the most intolerable thing he'd ever heard of. The superior was putting together a team of investigators and would send them to the institute very soon. The friend informed me that if I were indeed found to be deaf as accused, I would be disciplined as a bad example in front of all the others.

Some friends helped me get admitted to an inpatient medical facility for two weeks. I was healthy as a horse. Nevertheless, the staff checked me all over. Doctors were called in for consultation, but they could find nothing wrong, not even with a minor organ or tissue. They never did agree on a diagnosis, right up to the day I left. Oddly, though, they never got around to checking my hearing.

Meanwhile, the ruckus I had left behind at the institute evaporated before I was out of the hospital. My secretary, my chauffeur, Old Zhang from the front office, the department head who had written the note of concern about my health, and all my subordinates who professed a sense of justice expressed their righteous indignation against the slanderous accusations. In front of the investigators they ticked off example after example to prove that I was by no means deaf. "How could a deaf person advocate appreciating music and making listening to it an all-day habit?" they asked. "How could a deaf person mediate an argument in a public place?" as I had done at the theater. "How could a deaf person listen to an old subordinate discuss a personal difficulty and then promise to consider the request? *Deaf*? What a joke!" People stated that such slander insulted not only the new director but also every officer and worker at the institute. Could anyone imagine that the associates and subordinates could really be so blind as not to see that their director was deaf? Wasn't it strange that the *gang* with ulterior motives was the only one to see that the director was deaf!

Then my wife went to the institute and raised hell. She demanded that the team of investigators expose the gang and its ulterior motives and restore my good name. The investigators had to talk her out of resorting to even more drastic measures.

The day the investigating team left, it announced that the accusations in the jointly signed letter were false and indicated nothing more than the gloomy hearts of the signatories. Further, such conduct was not respectable and should come to a stop.

The first day I got back to the institute, I called an all-staff meeting and made a three-minute speech:

"Comrades: I came here to the institute today directly from the hospital. I have learned that during the two weeks I was away, something rather unpleasant happened. What was it?—I'd rather not get into it at this time. The only thing I want to tell you is this: I am not deaf, although on many occasions I do wish I were. The deaf do not have to listen to anything they don't want to hear, do they? Isn't it true that there aren't a whole lot of words in this world that are actually worth the trouble hearing? As for the unfortunate events that occurred in my absence, I'd rather let things blow over like a forgettable gust of wind . . . a joke, or prank, but bearing no ill will. Write it off as what they like to call black humor. We have enough stress in our lives, and a sense of humor never hurt anyone. And black humor, as the Americans say, is the highest form of humor."

People started to laugh.

I glanced out over the faces and saw them involved in all kinds of laughter, but I kept my demeanor serious. My dear readers, we both know I had become adept at what I was doing. At that particular moment I positively reveled in my enjoyment—the enjoyment of deception.

That afternoon I received a letter. It was from that out-of-town deaf man I had helped—no, *deceived*—on the bus. Here is what he had written:

Dear Director Liang:

How have you been? I was so glad to meet you on the bus. You let me believe again that the spirit of Lei Feng is alive and will always be alive in our society.

Although I didn't find that qigong *practitioner who can cure deafness, although I'm still deaf—please do not think I've been disappointed. No, I was not the least bit disappointed! You see, I am on a lifelong quest. It goes beyond trying to cure my deafness. Had I found the* qigong *practitioner—had he really restored my hearing—all my aspirations in life would have vanished with the deafness. Getting my hearing restored is the only thing I have to look forward to in life. If a man ends up without any aspirations, why, his spirit will wither away. From that point of view, I hope I will be deaf forever. Then I'll always be able to cherish the hope of having my hearing restored, to cherish the search for the person who may be able to restore my hearing. My life will forever be spurred onward by the hope of fulfilling my dream of finding the one who can cure me.*

The truth is I'm used to being deaf. You couldn't know that deafness has marvelous advantages. For example, when the Cultural Revolution had people all over the country searching their minds, they completely left me out of it. What was a mighty tempest to others was a time of tranquility for me. It started silently, went on for ten years silently, and ended silently. During the Cultural Revolution, the rebel leaders in my work unit took special care of me. They excused me from the slogan-shouting assemblies. So I never joined in shouting any slogan, not even "Long live Chairman Mao!" For all I knew, I could have blurted out some reactionary slogan instead. Needless to say, I never "Down with!"-ed or "Safeguard!"-ed anybody. If I was never on the winning side, at least I never ended up on the wrong side. After the Cultural Revolution when a lot of people were being told to "clarify themselves," I never had to explain anything. I was innocent—crystal clear—all because I was deaf.

No doubt you are a good person. I will pray to God every day that one day you will go deaf.

I am a devout Christian. Although I know that God doesn't really exist, the one person worth believing in, if you stop and think about it, could only be God.

May God bring you good luck!

Yours,

Anonymous

His letter left me pondering for a whole hour. I chain-smoked half a pack of cigarettes.

Then I burned the letter.

I did not write a reply, and not just because the writer was anonymous, either. I felt no inclination to write him back.

I found myself filled with disgust for the out-of-town deaf man, but mingled with that was some odd feeling of gratitude. His letter tantalized me with hints of some vague enlightenment. I couldn't be certain, though; perhaps it was seducing me into some otherworldly realm of thought.

Anyway, it was from about that time that I decided that I simply must find someone who could cure my deafness. I didn't care whether it was a *qigong* specialist or an unpardonable devil. I really didn't expect to be cured, either, but I was convinced that I had to try.

I secretly visited a *qigong* practitioner in the city. At first he completely denied that he could cure deafness, saying that I was misinformed about him.

I told him they had printed the story in the evening newspaper. Obviously somebody wanted to spread the word about his medical skills. I then showed him the yellowing newspaper article.

He didn't even bother to look at it. He wrote on a pad that, frankly, the newspaper reporter who interviewed him was the daughter of his friend. New on the job. With the best of intentions, she had brought him a lot of trouble. He went on to recount the time, when Mao Zedong was still alive, that he had confided to the American reporter Edgar Snow right there on the rostrum at Tian An Men that the cult of personality was a pain in the ass, even if it might be necessary sometimes. The specialist continued that he repeated to the girl just what he had told the American reporter—that a great leader can be a mediocrity in some aspects, and the same applied to *qigong* experts, too.

As for me, it was the practitioner's business whether he wanted to get into the personality cult or not. It was the American reporter's business if he wanted to follow up on the effects of propaganda or not—just as it was the newspaper readers' business if they chose to believe what they read or not. What it all came down to is that we all have our own perspective on things. I, the specialist pointed out, shouldn't have taken the report so seriously.

He seemed to be telling me that I had made a fool of myself. Still, I wasn't ready to give up. I begged him to try to do something, anything. He didn't refuse and soon was applying his *qigong* procedure to each ear half an hour at a time.

After an hour working at this, his head oozed with sweat, but the world was still silent to me, absolutely silent.

He shook his head and indicated with a facial expression and a shrug that nothing could be done. He wrote on the pad: *Please get someone better qualified.*

I started to laugh.

He regarded me for a while with a strange look on his face. Finally, I burst into uncontrolled laughter.

He wrote another sentence on the pad: *Why do you laugh?*

I collected myself and said, "Don't you *qigong* experts always say, 'To work together, let us link our hearts together first'? Perhaps I didn't have enough faith."

He then wrote: *The tree branches welcome all migrating birds, whether from south or north. The leaves deliver winds from east and west. Our society has no faith anymore, let alone the individual people. You and I have spent some time together playing at qigong. We can go on if it's enjoyable or stop if it isn't. But my rules are that we don't take the game so seriously that we get mad at each other.*

I had enough sense to know it was time to leave—and yet my compulsion to find something worth believing in grew ever stronger.

One evening my son showed me his first essay he had ever written for school. The title left me dumbfounded for quite a while: "On My Daddy Being Not Deaf."

He had written:

In my daddy's institute somebody started a rumor that my dad is deaf. Whether he is or is not deaf I think I know better than anyone else. I know my father is definitely not deaf. This is the hard, true fact. To doubt this is to doubt the hard, true facts. If we do not want to believe the truth, what else in this world can we believe? Long live the truth!

The teacher's comment on the essay was "Clear-cut premise, logical conclusion. Commendable: connected your daddy's being not deaf to belief in factual truth, thus more serious and significant."

To reward my son, I gave him one yuan and permission to invite some friends to go watch a movie at the video store.

After our son left, my wife and I looked at each other for a while without saying anything. Then we began a written conversation that lasted for two hours.

After all was written and done, we came to the same conclusion: our son had figured out that I was deaf, but he refused to accept the hard, true facts. We had never acted to deceive him. We simply wanted to hide the awful truth from him. He deceived himself and was proud of it. He had deceived himself so thoroughly that he didn't even realize what he had done. We were both quite worried about him. What should we do?

I have to say that my wife was ahead of me on this point. She told me that the husband of one of her coworkers was a specialist in otology, in fact, the city's leading authority in otology. She insisted on taking me to see him the next day. She wrote that if my hearing was restored just a little bit, then my *un*deafness would become a "hard, true fact." My deafness then would be forgotten as if it had never happened. Our son's essay would of course be a good and true essay, and his teacher's comments would be something we could honestly be proud of. Since this matter concerned the education of our next generation, we both were willing to put aside our recent, minor differences and focus on the big picture.

The next day I called in sick with a stomachache and set

out with my wife to see the otologist. He gave me a respectful, thorough examination, after which he consulted privately with my wife for a long time. He might as well have talked to her in front of me, of course. In a hospital the deaf would like to be considered deaf as a courtesy if nothing else. In other places, of course, such as my institute, it was a totally different story.

When they were finished and my wife returned, I noticed that she looked blue in the face.

On our way out through the waiting room, I was astonished to see quite a few people from my institute seated on the long bench among the other patients! There was the department head who had written the note of concern about my health. There was Old Zhang from the front office, and some other colleagues, and . . . even my secretary! Each of them was holding a radio/tape cassette player and wearing a headset. Some of them smiled and nodded at me, as if we shared some tacit understanding. Others adopted an avoidance stare in order not to risk eye contact with me. My secretary was the most natural of all, smiling ingenuously as if it were the most ordinary thing in the world for the two of us to have our ears checked at the same time in the same clinic.

As soon as my wife and I got home, I demanded that she tell me the otologist's diagnosis. She wrote three comments on a piece of paper:

> *According to the specialist, your ears are completely healthy. There is nothing organically wrong with them.*
>
> *What caused your hearing loss could be too much stress. Symptoms like yours usually don't need any treatment. After you calm down, the problem will go away by itself.*
>
> *However, in your case, since your deafness has gone on for so long, it could be more than just stress. You might have*

some kind of psychological block. The specialist came up with a special term for your symptoms: mentally selective exclusion. It's like if you really didn't want to see something, you could actually make yourself blind. Or if you wanted to lose your sense of smell, you really couldn't tell a fragrance from a stink.

Then she proceeded to interrogate me on paper.

You're going to have to tell me in no uncertain terms: Why did you wish yourself deaf? Perhaps you made things easier for yourself, but look at the trouble you've caused me. We've been husband and wife for all these years. I bore a son for you and brought him up. I have never been unfaithful to you. What did I do to deserve this from you?

By the time she was finished, she was sobbing bitterly.

I suddenly remembered the letter that the out-of-town deaf man sent me. So *this* was the powerful, seductive force playing upon my subconscious as I read the letter. I wanted to stab him in the chest.

THE NEXT MORNING, as I passed through the institute on the way to my office, I nodded to everyone I met and said, "Good morning," as was my custom. To the young I gave a pat on the shoulder; that's a better expression of friendliness than mere words. To the older ones I offered a cigarette and made some comment about the weather. Whatever they said in response was immaterial; I laughed merrily. That actually turned out to be a great way to keep some inconvenient issues under wraps. Readers, you may want to give this a try yourselves.

The ones that I had unexpectedly run into at the otology office the day before acted sheepish when they saw me. To my thinking, I was the one who should have been feeling awkward. Yet their behavior was unmistakable. Well, then, let them have their embarrassment. That spared me the necessity of disguising a guilty conscience.

I hung a "Do Not Disturb" sign on my office door and sat down to have a frank and serious discussion with my secretary. I opened: *To be? Or not to be?*

She stared at me for a moment, then wrote: *Bodhi is not a true tree. Bright mirror is not the dresser. Why do you have to make everything so serious?*

We are two grasshoppers tied with one string.

Yes—for honor and for disgrace.

I wrote: *The sea of bitterness has no bounds. Repent, said the Buddha, and the shore is at hand.*

The shore already is at hand. So then why would you need to repent?

You mean . . . I should keep on?

She wrote: *If you don't consider yourself deaf, then who could? Not to mention that we have more and more officers here coming down with "mentally selective exclusion" to some degree or other. Some of them look but don't see. Some listen but don't hear. Some keep quiet but they aren't thinking about anything. Some talk but never do anything. It used to be "The monk does his devotions some days and tolls the bell other days"; nowadays, you can get away with just doing one or the other. They would even think you were a better monk if you focused on less! How in the world else do you think you could have gotten this far without catching hell? Look, if you weren't deaf and you had to face all those people applying for housing, or getting jobs for their* children, or asking for a raise or a promotion, the ones filing for a divorce, or arguing with their neighbors, the bellyachers just looking for something to whine about or a chance to blow off some steam—would you be able to show anything like the terrific self-control that you've kept so far, and so successfully?

I wrote: Your words educate me better than ten years of schooling.

So do yours.

How I wish we had met earlier.

Translator's Postscript

LIANG XIAOSHENG HAS been a respected writer in China since his novella *This Is a Miraculous Land* won the annual All-China Short Novel Prize in 1982. Developing his craft patiently, while employed in the well-respected Beijing Film Studio and later the Beijing Children's Film Studio, Liang is today one of China's most popular writers. Nevertheless, except for a few short stories, Liang Xiaosheng's work is unknown among non-readers of Chinese.

Liang Xiaosheng was born in 1949 in Harbin, the provincial capital of Heilongjiang (formerly Manchuria), in northeastern China. His father, a construction worker, could barely provide for the family, which subsisted on steamed corn bread and wild herbs in a hovel shared with several other families. The Cultural Revolution intruded upon and forever altered Liang's expectations for the future. In 1968 his high-school studies ended when he and most of his classmates, as "educated youth," were sent to the Great Northern Wasteland to work on desolate communes. There Liang discovered true poverty; he could no longer pity himself as one of the unluckiest youths in the world. Liang worked at various tasks—assisting a land-reclamation project, teaching elementary school, and writing for the local newspaper. The daily hardships coupled with the opportunity to develop writing skills eventually enabled Liang to compose *This Is a Miraculous Land, The Growth Ring,* and *Blizzard at Midnight,* masterpieces that graphically portray extreme sacrifices extracted from his generation.

The turning point in Liang's life occurred in 1974. The Cultural Revolution had run its course and universities were beginning to revive; Liang was admitted into the Department of Chinese Language at Fudan University in Shanghai. Upon graduation in 1977 he was assigned to the Beijing Film Studio. At that time Liang began to write in earnest, turning out a novel nearly once every year.

Since winning the All-China Short Novel Prize, Liang Xiaosheng has garnered dozens of national awards and recognition throughout China. Though largely unknown outside of his country, Liang has a high profile among Chinese readers as a former Red Guard and rusticated intellectual youth who stands for and stands by his generation. Liang's 1988 novel, *Confessions of a Red Guard,* sheds tragic, and sometimes bawdy and witty, light on the travails of this group.

In *Panic* and *Deaf,* Liang turns his focus toward his generation's contemporary predicament. The protagonists in both stories move through roughly the same morass of petty corruption, bureaucratic backbiting, and opportunistic adultery. Liang uses satire to express the financial and sexual frustration, pathetic mediocrity, and impotent resentment of aging "educated youth" now trapped in a socialist economy whose relevance is rapidly being upstaged by the brash economic dynamism of a new entrepreneurial class.

By tapping into universal human concerns and personality

types recognizable to those of us in the West, Liang further opens our window onto Chinese society. In these two stories, he does so in a tone that is deceptively light and humorous.

Also available in the series

The Three-Inch Golden Lotus
BY FENG JICAI
Translated by David Wakefield

The Remote Country of Women
BY BAI HUA
Translated by Qingyun Wu and Thomas O. Beebee

Chaos and All That
BY LIU SOLA
Translated by Richard King

Family Catastrophe
BY WANG WEN-HSING
Translated by Susan Wan Dolling

Imperfect Paradise
BY SHEN CONGWEN
Edited by Jeffrey Kinkley

Virgin Widows
BY GU HUA
Translated by Howard Goldblatt

The Past and the Punishments
BY YU HUA
Translated by Andrew F. Jones

Shanghai Express
BY ZHANG HENSHUI
Translated by William A. Lyell

Snake's Pillow and Other Stories
BY ZHU LIN
Translated by Richard King

The Money Demon
BY CHEN DIEXIAN
Translated by Patrick Hanan

Blades of Grass: The Stories of Lao She
BY LAO SHE
Translated by William A. Lyell and Sarah Wei-ming Chen